TIA'AHLEE'S STORY

A CHILD of FAITH

Tia'Ahlee Maxie

RIVER GROVE
BOOKS

This book is a memoir reflecting the author's present recollections of experiences over time. Its story and its words are the author's alone. Some details and characteristics may be changed, some events may be compressed, and some dialogue may be recreated.

Published by River Grove Books
Austin, TX
www.rivergrovebooks.com

Copyright © 2023 Tia'Ahlee Maxie

All rights reserved.

Thank you for purchasing an authorized edition of this book and for complying with copyright law. No part of this book may be reproduced, stored in a retrieval system, or transmitted by any means, electronic, mechanical, photocopying, recording, or otherwise, without written permission from the copyright holder.

Distributed by River Grove Books

Design and composition by Greenleaf Book Group
Cover design by Greenleaf Book Group
Cover images used under license from
©Shutterstock.com/kikk; ©Shutterstock.com/Artem Musaev
Interior images used under license from
©Shutterstock.com/Wirestock Creators

Publisher's Cataloging-in-Publication data is available.

Print ISBN: 978-1-63299-683-1

eBook ISBN: 978-1-63299-684-8

First Edition

Dear Grandma Dolpha,

Although I didn't get to meet you in person, you are always with me in Spirit because she is one of my guardian angels.

When people say mean things, it really hurts me because I am different. It's really sad because we're all people. We're no different. If you have cancer, heart defects, or any other health condition love who you are. Because you're not going through this struggle for the world. You are going through it for you and the good Lord. No one else matters. Only you and God. I thank God for keeping me in His hands and helping me recover. I'm still here. And I thank God every day for that.

—Tia'Ahlee Maxie
July 3, 2020

Contents

Preface: **The Angels Among Us** ix

Part 1: Amazing Grace, How Sweet the Sound

Chapter 1: **Made Perfect in Weakness.** 3

Chapter 2: **The Power of Christ** 17

Chapter 3: **I Will Boast All the More Gladly** 35

Part 2: 'Twas Grace That Taught My Heart to Fear

Chapter 4: **When I Came to You** 45

Chapter 5: **In Fear and Much Trembling** 51

Chapter 6: **I Was with You in Weakness** 61

Chapter 7: **In Demonstration of the Spirit—Spending Time with Grandma Dolpha.** 93

Chapter 8: **My Speech and My Message.** 107

Chapter 9: **The Testimony of God** 117

Part 3: And Grace My Fears Relieved

Chapter 10: **Do Not Let Your Hearts Be Troubled** 129

Chapter 11: **My Peace I Give to You** 137

Epilogue: **Bright Shining as the Sun** 147

Appendix: **Artwork, Poetry, and Photos** 149

About the Author. 157

Preface

The Angels Among Us

Hello, my name is Tia'Ahlee. I am a sixteen-year-old girl, and I'm here to tell you about my life.. My full name means "strong-willed" in English and "prophetic bird" in Arabic, and it also means "to ascend and to stand in Heaven in health." I think my parents named me well because, in some ways, I am like a bird. I'm light and small and love looking up at the sky like birds do. I feel a connection with them because they are gentle spirits and tiny angels with wings.

I also like cats. I have two boy cats, one of which is named Shadow. He is black and has reddish stripes. And the other's name is Rody; he is a gray kitty with black tiger stripes. They bring me and my sister a lot of joy.

A Child of Faith

Shadow (top) and Rody (bottom), relaxing outside

But I'm not perfect. I can be stubborn sometimes. Sometimes, my mother and I argue, but it's not a big argument when we do. It's more stuff like wanting to play when it's time to do homework or not putting on my oxygen (because I don't like using it) when my tongue is purple. But I am also strong like my mother and very kind like her, too. She and my father and sister love me very much, just as I love them.

My parents tell me I'm supposed to be here and that I'm one of God's angels sent to Earth to help other people. And it always makes me smile and feel proud when she says that, because I love angels and helping people too. My path is not an easy one, but it is the one that was chosen for me. My mom says if I couldn't handle this road, I wouldn't be on it. So, every

Preface

day, I take it one step at a time, and that's why I'm here telling my story, so you know what it's like being born an angel to do God's work.

I sometimes get messages from God and Jesus when I am struggling. These messages guide and comfort me. My mom calls me an angel because I am always giving to others and praying, like her, for others. She also says I am her miracle baby and that God sent her to me so I could share my messages with the world. She also tells me I'm on borrowed time, because my health is challenging me. But I have a close relationship with God, and I know when my time comes, I will ascend into Heaven and be in perfect health and with all my angels. So I am very brave and feel blessed to be here with my family and also to have that connection with God and my angels at the same time.

I am sixteen years old now. And I really believe I am here today by the grace of God and the love and determination of my apostle and pastor, my doctors, and all the people in my church and family—like my sister, Talia (Le Le)—who pray for me and support me every day.

Most people don't know this, but I have been bullied and abused most of my life. Others thought that because I was different from them, it was OK to do bad things to me. Now that I have the courage from my family and God, I no longer let others bully me. I still have trouble trusting people because of what happened. It was hard for me to experience the bullying

A Child of Faith

Me and my sister, Le Le, when she was just a baby

and abuse, and I never want it to happen again. But once I know I am safe, I will learn to trust you.

I hope you are not being bullied or abused like I was. But if you are, I want you to know you have just as much a right to be here as they do. And even if you have cancer, heart defects, or any other health condition that isn't your fault, you are perfect just the way you are. Other people may not understand you are special and were chosen to be their teacher. Because when we

Preface

are given gifts like ours, it is always for a reason. My reason is to give hope and healing to others. I am a child of faith because of my upbringing but also because that's the way God made me.

And I want you to know that God loves you, too. And no matter what others say or do to you, remember you are one of the angels among us. Please don't feel you are going through this alone. Your angels are there to comfort you, just as my angels do me. I don't want you to feel alone or scared when you are struggling. I wrote this book for you. I want this book to be like a conversation we are having. Just pretend I am here sitting next to you, telling you about my life. Some of it may be similar to yours. Some of it may be very different.

Something else I want you to know is that you do not need to keep your struggles secret. If someone is picking on you at school, tell your parents or your teacher. If someone is hurting you at home and you can't tell your parents, tell a close friend or the police. If you are told to keep quiet about anything from someone who is bullying you or abusing you, I want you to make as much noise as you can. Do you know why? Because you do not deserve to be treated this way. Bullies and mean people want you to keep quiet, to make you feel ashamed and scared so they can keep doing bad things to you. Don't give them that power over you; it's not theirs to take!

Whatever is happening to you right now, please remember you are always protected and blessed. This book is my prayer for you. I wrote every page to give you hope, love, and strength so

A Child of Faith

you can carry on with the important work that God has given *you* to do on this great earth.

Ever since I was six years old, my dream has been to write a book to share my message with people like you. When my mom told my doctors about my dream when I was fifteen, they wrote to Make-A-Wish to see if they could make my dream of becoming a published author come true. I was so happy when they did this. Not everyone gets picked. My mom didn't want me to get too excited, but I already knew I would be picked because God told me I would.

Even though I knew I would be picked, when my mom and I learned I had been selected to have my wish granted, I was so excited that I ran around my church seven times! Seven! Normally, I can't run because I have a heart condition, and my baseline oxygen is at 60 percent. When you have low oxygen, it is *really* hard to breathe—like, all the time. I cough sometimes, and some people give me a funny look like it's gross or something. Sometimes that makes me feel embarrassed because they don't understand how hard something they take for granted, like breathing, is for people like me. I *have* to breathe, just like they do. And coughing is how I can make room for air to reach me.

I also have an oxygen tank to help me, but sometimes I don't use it because I am embarrassed about what others will think if I wear it at school. I have been teased about it before at school. A lot. I still get funny looks when I wear it, so I go outside to

Preface

use my oxygen when I am at school. Just like the wheelchair I have to use. I get teased about that, too, because most kids don't understand why I need a wheelchair. I can walk, but I need to use it because I get tired and out of breath if I walk too far. I cannot help it if I cough or need a wheelchair or use oxygen. And the people that know me understand that. Sometimes I have to use my oxygen in public around strangers, and it takes a lot of courage because a lot of people think it's strange, and it makes me feel bad when they give me dirty looks.

One time, I made a video on TikTok to show others my oxygen tank and how I use it. I was embarrassed to show the whole world, but I still did it. In fact, it gave me a little more courage to use it, because now others will see the video and understand me a little more. If you have something you have to wear that makes you look different from other people, I get it. It can be really hard when people are making fun of you. But I want you to be brave and wear what you need. Your health is important. And if others don't understand or make fun of you, please remember that God wants you here, just like He wants me here.

I don't know if this is the case for you, but because of my immune system, I also have to wear a surgical mask like people did during COVID-19. I can't get sick from other people, and it is not an option for me to take it off. A lot of people aren't wearing masks anymore, which makes me look different. But my family wears a mask with me because they want me to be

A Child of Faith

healthy and safe from illness. I know this makes me sound frail. And in some ways, my body is. But in other ways, I am fierce like my mom. My Spirit is strong. My Spirit is always healthy, and it is here not just for me but also for you.

And sometimes, there are moments when the good Lord fills me with His love and grace, and it's like I'm all healed, and nothing can stop me. It's the best feeling in the whole world. I know this is why I'm here today. I am very blessed, because most kids like me don't live this long.

But I am still here, and this is my story.

—**Tia'Ahlee Maxie,
Lufkin, Texas**

Part 1

Amazing Grace, How Sweet the Sound

> But he said to me, "My grace is sufficient for you, for my power is made perfect in weakness." Therefore I will boast all the more gladly about my weaknesses, so that Christ's power may rest on me.
>
> —2 Corinthians 12:9, NIV

Chapter 1

Made Perfect in Weakness

Trials and tribulations
Are part of life for all.
Sometimes we get big ones—
Other times they are small.
Whenever they appear,
Don't fret or run away.
The Holy Spirit is with you.
And with you, He will stay.

—Tia'Ahlee Maxie

When my mom was pregnant with me, her current apostle told my mother that her pregnancy with me would be very difficult. He said she would go through many trials and tribulations with me when she was pregnant and when I was born, but that I would make it and that she needed to stay strong for both of us. I think he told her that so she could prepare for me. My mother was skeptical when she heard this because she had miscarried three other babies, so even though she was hoping I would be born, she didn't want to be disappointed. Again.

But miracles happen every day. Like me, my apostle knows things. It's like he sees the future before it happens or something. I get that knowing feeling, too. My mother says when I was little, I used to call my apostle and his wife Mr. Jesus and Mrs. Mary. His wife also has a very close relationship with God and is the pastor of our church. Everyone thought that was cute when I would call them Jesus and Miss Jesus. But I really meant it. They are so close to God it's like being right there with Jesus and Mother Mary. I love them so much, and they comfort me and my family when we are going through trying times.

They are like family. Sometimes they even come to the house and pray for us. When we go to church, they always hug me and my younger sister, Le Le. We have a very special relationship with them. They pray for us every day.

My mom will call them when we need extra prayers, and they always pray for us. One time when I was little, I was getting surgery at Texas Children's Hospital, and the pastor took the time to pray for me. And that's exactly what she did.

Chapter 1

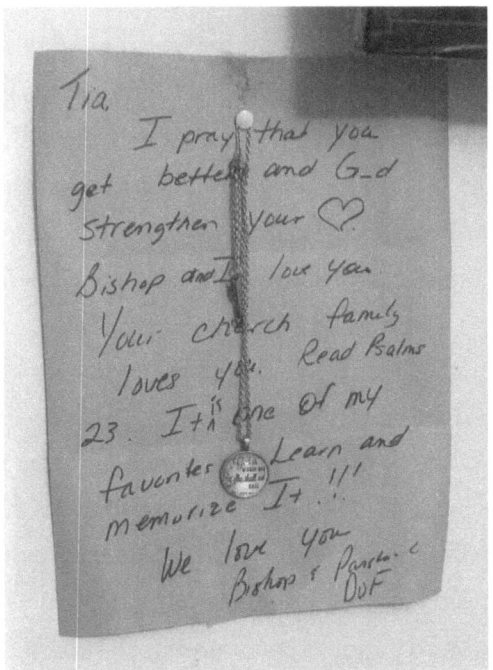

The letter and pendant from our pastor

After she finished praying, she wrote a letter to me and brought me a pendant that I sometimes wear. I still have the letter and pendant on the wall in my bedroom. They are very special to me and helped me get through a risky surgery.

Whenever I see the letter and pendant, I smile and give thanks to God for her and my apostle. We are very blessed to have them in our lives.

• • •

A Child of Faith

My mother remembers early in her pregnancy, when she went to the doctor to see if I was going to be a boy or a girl, the doctor took a picture of me inside her womb. And she says I was smiling right at the camera. She says she knew right then that I would be a happy baby. My mom says if you look real close, you can see me smile. I like that picture, but I wonder: How did I know to smile like that when I was so small?

Even though I was smiling inside my mom's belly, it was a rough start getting here—for both of us! She says I kicked her good in the doctor's office one day when she was in her ninth month with me, and my heart rate went up to 230 beats per minute! My mom says it really hurt when I kicked her, and the doctor said that was very uncommon for a baby to have such a high heart rate. My mom took some deep breaths and continued listening to classical music because it was very soothing for her (and me, too!). But when my mother was trying to relax, I kicked her hard again, and my heartbeat was just a little lower at 215 beats per minute. I think the music helped a little, but the kick still hurt my mother.

The nurse was about to adjust the belt over my mom on the exam room table when I kicked her a third time. When she said, "Ouch!" the doctor sent us to the hospital right next to their clinic. My mother knew something wasn't right. When she was at the hospital, they ran some lab work and then sent us home and told her to rest because they weren't sure what was going on. The doctor said if she started having more pain

Chapter 1

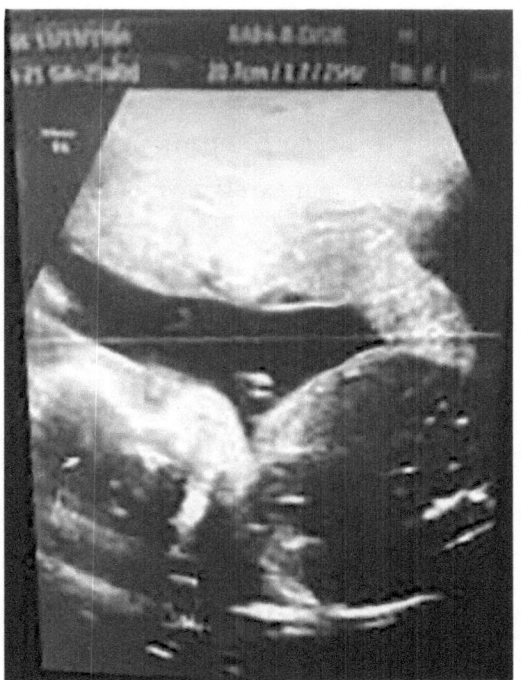

Can you see me smiling?

or false labor to come back. But my mother got some rest and went to work the very next day.

The Day I Was Born

The week before I was born, the doctor said I was high risk and that my mom should watch for sharp pain or labor pain. They said if that happened, she needed to go to the hospital right away. But my mom was so busy working (even at nine months pregnant!) that she didn't notice when I kept kicking her that day. The day I was born, she had to fight hard, not just for me but for herself, too. At the time, my mother was working as an accounts manager for a repo company, and they had to get a truck that someone wasn't making payments on. The man told my mother to come with him, which she thought was strange because she worked in the office. But she went anyway.

When they got there, the man who was supposed to repossess the truck was too chicken to get out of the car because there was a giant white dog outside by the truck. My mom says it looked like a Great Dane mixed with a wolf. He told my mom to get out of the car instead, which made her upset.

She told the man *he* was there to repo the truck, but he wouldn't move, even though it was his job. This dog was scary looking, too. But it takes a lot to scare my mom, and she wasn't going to let a dog stop her. So she got out of the car with her giant pregnant belly, ignored the big dog, and jumped up on the bed of a diesel truck. She climbed in between the back seat, belly first, with one leg and her giant belly, to make her way to the front seat to hook up the hitch so they could take the car.

Can you believe that? I mean, my mom was nine months pregnant with me, and she did all that. She just kept going. Because that's how she is. She even risked getting hurt by that dog, but my mom never gives up. She always tells me and my baby sister, Le Le, to never give up. I think that's why I'm still here and why I plan on staying.

When my mom and the other guy finished with the truck,

Chapter 1

they were walking back to the office. That is when someone slapped my mom on the back of the head. When she turned around, she saw it was her ex's ex-girlfriend. My mother was very shocked. You would be too. That lady slapped my mom so hard it made her head bounce forward. My mom says she told the woman to leave her alone, but the woman started yelling at her. While pregnant with me, my mom slapped her back, knocking her down, and called the police.

And then that same lady told the cops that my mom hit *her*. That lady lied to the police to get my mother in trouble because she was jealous of my mother. My mom is pretty, and that other lady didn't like that my mom used to be with her boyfriend. But that's not my mom's fault, and it's no reason to go hitting someone across the back of the head.

I was sitting there in my mom's tummy, kicking and wiggling, ready to be born, but she didn't have time to notice she was in labor because she was fighting just to get through her day. After that mean lady hit her, my mom had to go make a statement at the sheriff's office. Fortunately, some people saw the mean lady slap my mom. So my mom didn't go to jail. (I knew she wouldn't. My mom's too good for jail.)

When my mother finally got back to her car, she noticed she was cramping really badly. But she didn't think much of it because she had real bad cramping all during her pregnancy with me. I feel bad that my mom had such a hard time that day. But even then, she didn't quit. She drove herself straight to the hospital after all that. She didn't think it was anything, but they wanted to admit her because I was supposed to be born in just a few days. My mom didn't want to stay, but they finally convinced her because the cramps were so bad. My mother says as soon as she got to her room, her water broke, and it was time for me to be born.

For eight hours that day, my mom was in labor with me, but she didn't realize it because the Devil was distracting her with a repo man, a giant dog, and a mean lady. And it didn't stop there. After I was born, the nurses kept wanting to take me back to the nursery, but my mom wouldn't let them. She just knew something wasn't right. And she said no every day for two days in a row. Even to the doctors! She said she just wanted to hold me and see how pretty I was.

When she said no on the second day after I was born, an alarm went off on the pregnancy ward, and my mom asked what that was about. One of the nurses said the hospital was on lockdown because there was a nurse stealing babies! And when they asked to take me back to the nursery after that, my mom still refused. And I'm glad she did. I wouldn't want to be with another mother because I love mine so much.

I like that about my mom. She always knows when something isn't right. She also knows when something is. On the third day we were there, my mom's cousin was working and got my mom to finally let them take me to the nursery so they could examine me. She made her cousin promise to check in

Chapter 1

on me often, to watch over me, and to let my mom know how I was doing.

My mother says I was very tiny, even though I was full-term. I weighed four pounds and ten ounces, so the doctors were very concerned because I should have weighed almost twice that. When I was in the nursery, they noticed I had a heart murmur and that I was turning blue because I wasn't getting enough oxygen.

Emergency Surgery

When my mom woke up the next morning, she was getting dressed and ready to take me home. But then the doctor came in and said he needed to talk to her about my condition. My mom was like, "Condition?" The doctor told her my case was very rare. He said he normally didn't work with kids on Medicaid, but this was a special case. He told my mother that I had a heart murmur. However, there was something else wrong. He said they had been testing me overnight, and I had turned a little blue because my oxygen levels were so low. The murmur wasn't closing up like they hoped it would. On top of that, I had a leaky valve. It was a very complex case. I think my mom was in shock, trying to take it all in. She thought she was going to take me home, and now she was hearing I was turning blue.

My mom wondered if she was going to lose me, too, just like her other babies. The doctor understood my mother's pain, but he was also firm with her because I was very sick. He said, "At this point, it's life or death. To save her life, your daughter needs to go right now."

My mother just watched the words come out of his mouth, still processing what he was saying, like he was talking in slow motion or something. And then the doctor said, "I want you to see her before we go, so you can say goodbye."

Goodbye?

This woke my mom up from her shock.

"What's happening?" my mom asked while fighting back tears.

The doctor said my oxygen levels were dropping very fast and that I had a very serious condition and needed to be flown immediately to Texas Children's Hospital in Houston, which is about three hours away. He said I may need heart surgery that very day.

How could this be happening? Is this what her apostle meant by tribulations? My mom started to cry when she remembered he had told her this.

They wheeled me into my mother's room in an incubator before rushing me to the helicopter and said she had to sign papers to approve the treatment. Between tears, my mom signed the papers and then looked at me. Her apostle had said I would be OK. She had to trust in him and Jesus that everything would be all right. She looked down. The incubator had these little gloves for her to reach inside to touch me.

Chapter 1

She said she was very sad but still wanted to let me know she was there. So she reached in and touched my little hands with the special gloves. She wished she could hold on to my little hands forever, but they told her it was time to go.

But my mom wasn't going to give up on me. She even tried to ride with me on the helicopter, but she passed out because, back then, she was terrified of flying. So the helicopter flew me to the hospital, and my mom drove and beat the helicopter by twenty-five minutes! I'm serious. My mother doesn't let anything stop her when it comes to her children. Not even traffic. She's like a mama lion. She protects me and my baby sister fiercely and will not stop protecting us. Ever.

When I arrived, my mom met with the heart doctor. She asked him if he prayed, and he said no, so my mom said she did not want someone who did not believe in God to operate on me. So she asked for a different doctor. They found another doctor and brought him to my mom, and she asked him if he believed in God, and he said yes. Then she asked if he and the other doctors and nurses would pray for her and Tia when he was in the operating room, and he said yes. He said he was just getting off his shift, but he would be happy to help Tia. My mother knew this was the right doctor for me. So, while she was praying for me, my doctor, the nurses, and the whole surgical team were praying for me and my mother. I'm so glad she asked for the right doctor. He saved my life and my mother's, too, because she was scared, and it was very hard for her to see me struggling. She couldn't take losing another baby. And I was going to fight as hard as I could for her.

The cardiologist did emergency open-heart surgery on me that day and discovered I was born without a pulmonary artery. You need a pulmonary artery to live. Without one, you can't get oxygen to your lungs. So he added a Blalock-Taussig (BT) shunt to serve as my pulmonary artery so I could breathe. The doctor told her they had to give me a lot of blood during my surgery, because I had lost so much blood when they operated on me. I am sure that was stressful for her. She thought she was going to have a baby and then take me home, and here I was, four days old, having open-heart surgery. They had to cut me open, and I was in the operating room for more than six hours. My mom said it may have been closer to eight. But she knew she had picked the right doctor. He was a man of faith and would pray for me so I could live.

The surgery was successful. We were there for several days while I recovered. My mom told me that she prayed for me every day. My god-aunt, who is her cousin, TaRhonda, was there with her for support. My mom told me that on the fifth day at Texas Children's Hospital, she got robbed, but they didn't get much because when my mother was young, her mom had always taught her to put her money and her ID in her bra. Because she had done that, all they had gotten were her purse and some paperwork. Her car keys were with the valet, and

Chapter 1

everything else she needed was tucked neatly inside her bra. So, while it was traumatic, it could have been worse.

When it was time to go home, the doctor explained how the shunt would work and what care I would need at home, like oxygen and medications. They said I would need to come back to be examined further and that I would need additional surgeries.

Additional surgeries?

My mother listened closely and shuffled through all the additional paperwork they gave her. The doctor explained that my heart was on the right side of my chest instead of my left, so everything was flipped. Because of that and all my other medical conditions, this was just the beginning of my medical care.

It was going to be a long journey. Like our apostle said, many trials and tribulations. But all would be OK. I know my angels were there that day they operated on me, because I survived. And my mom also looked down at me and smiled, because she knew it too.

Chapter 2

The Power of Christ

The power of Christ lives in me.
He's with me all day long.
The power of Christ lives in you.
He's there to make you strong.
The power of Christ lives in us.
How could it ever be,
That we should doubt His power,
Our Lord, His Majesty?

—Tia'Ahlee Maxie

When my mother was three months pregnant with me, she told her ex and my daddy that one of them was my father. She wasn't sure who the father was because she had broken up with my dad for a bit and gone back to her ex. My mom is an honest person and wanted them both to know so they could be there when she had me. My real dad was glad to hear that my mom was pregnant. He said even if he wasn't the biological father, he would always be there for me and take care of me. He even helped my mother get ready and bought her a stroller and other things she needed before I came into this world.

Her ex, on the other hand, was angry. Real angry. He yelled at my mom and came over to her place and beat her while she was pregnant with me. He was so mad because he was seeing someone else, and now, he had this "problem" to deal with. But he was also mad because he is just all kinds of mean.

It's a miracle that I was even born, given my mom had all those miscarriages before me, and her ex was beating on her all the time. Mostly in the face and arms. I don't think he kicked her in the stomach, but you would have to ask her that. It's not something I really like to talk about because I love my dad and am so glad that my mom eventually demanded a second paternity test, because it proved that Pat was my daddy and not the mean man.

When my mom was in the hospital and the first paternity results came in, they were inconclusive because I had received so much blood after I was born to keep me alive. Because of this, my mother's ex still insisted he was the father and that his name should be on the birth certificate. My mom and her ex fought over that. It was crazy because my mom just had me. I was her first baby to live. Shouldn't they just be happy for me? It didn't make sense to my mom or my dad that there was so

Chapter 2

much drama over this. My real dad said he would do right by my mom and take care of us either way. It didn't matter to him if I was his or not. But it did to the mean man.

I want you to know that even though I am sharing these painful events my parents went through, it is not to get your pity. Please do not feel sorry for us. We are strong, and events like this only pull us closer together. I am sharing this with you so that you know you are not alone. Bad things happen to good people, but that does not mean they deserve it or are bad people themselves. Sometimes life is challenging, and this was one of those times.

While my mom and her ex were fighting over who the real dad was, he started choking her because he said he should be on the birth certificate. My dad walked in on that in the hospital and was real upset because he saw him hurting my mom. So they started getting into it. One of the nurses came in and said my dad and my mom's ex couldn't be in there. And even though he wasn't my real dad (later on, the second test results proved that Pat was my real dad), my mom's ex said he was the real father and wasn't going to leave until his name was on the birth certificate. My dad left because he didn't want to upset my mom.

When everyone left, my mother tried to reason with him about the results being inconclusive and that they should wait. Then he started choking her again. And when he saw the nurse coming, he stopped, and they both signed the birth certificate in front of the nurse. My mom didn't feel she had any other choice. If she kept fighting it, she knew he would kill her after the nurse left. While the nurse was in the room, my mom was coughing from all the choking and rubbing her neck from the pain, but the nurse didn't notice. However, the next day my mom's social worker came by to see how she was doing and saw my mom's ex beating her hard in the face. Well, when the social worker saw that, she told him to stop and made him leave.

After we got home from the hospital, my mother's troubles weren't over. They were just beginning. Her ex would come to the apartment we had and start hitting my mom while I was playing with my toys. This made me cry. Hard. When this happened, my mom wanted to give me oxygen because when I cried like that, I would turn blue, and she could see my tongue was purple from across the room. One time it got real bad, and she kept saying she needed to give me oxygen, but her ex tried to stop her as he watched me turn bluer and bluer in the face. This made my mom mad.

She'd had enough of the choking and needed to get to me, or I would die. The only way she could get him to stop was to kick him hard in the balls. She thought that would stop him, but when he got up, he came after her, screaming. By then, my mom was furious, so she hit him over the head with a flat-screen TV to stop him from hurting her or me. Then she called 911, but they wouldn't come. The police get too many calls like

Chapter 2

that in our neighborhood, so they tend to look the other way. And it didn't help that my mom's ex was a volunteer policeman.

My mother's ex came another time and punched her in the jaw when she was trying to get away with me in the car. My mom was taking me to the store, and he was angry. She was taking him to court that week to get my real dad's name put on my birth certificate since the second paternity test proved that the mean man was not my real daddy. So, as my mom was putting me in the car seat, he grabbed her, punched her hard in the jaw, and called her all kinds of mean names. I started crying because he was hurting my mother, but I couldn't do anything. Crying was all I knew back then. My mom wiped her tears after he left and told me it was OK. She took me out of the car seat and rocked me back and forth in the back seat to comfort me. When we both stopped crying, she put me back in the seat, and we went to get groceries.

When my mom was in court with my dad, her ex still insisted he was the real father, even though the paternity test showed otherwise. I mean, 99.99 percent pretty much says you're the father. When we won the case, my mother and father were so happy.

It showed us that angels are never far away.

This was a lot for my mom to go through with me. I mean, she was a new mom—finally—after all these years. And now that she had a baby of her very own, she was fighting every day to keep her ex away and to keep me alive. I can't imagine the pain and heartache and stress it put on her. Soon after this started, she started having abdominal pain and had to see her OB-GYN. During the visit, they took some cultures, and when the results came in from the lab, they called my mom and asked her to come in.

My mother was diagnosed with ovarian cancer. While she was fighting for my life, she was now also fighting for hers. She was so stressed and miserable that she didn't even want to live. It was such a rough time for my mom. At one point, she told a social worker she wanted to die so all this pain would be over. It was a hard thing to say, but my mom didn't really want to be dead and decided she needed to confide in someone to keep her safe. My mother asked the social worker to get our apostle. When he visited my mom, she told him what was happening and asked him to pray for her so she would get better. He said of course he would, and slowly my mom started to feel better.

During this time, my mom was letting my dad and her ex both visit me. I'm sure it was hard on my dad to see my mom all bruised up like that. But he kept on visiting and tried to make it work to keep the peace. My mother only took one week off after she had me and then went right back to work. She had to. She didn't get paid leave, and we needed the money. But soon after we got home from the hospital, we had to go back because I was having complications and needed to get checked often to adjust my medication and schedule new procedures. And then, when I was starting to feel a little

Chapter 2

better, it was my mother's turn to have surgery to get rid of the ovary that had the cancer.

This made my mom's boss real upset because my mother had to take so much time off from work for me. He flat-out told her it was me or the job. So she chose me. My mom tells me that I saved her life. Because of me, she wanted to live, even though she was still getting beaten up by her ex while she was trying to recover from her surgery. Me and Daddy are the reason my mom broke up with him.

I think my mom would have kept putting up with her ex had it not been for me and my daddy. Even though my mom tried to keep the peace with her ex to keep him happy, there was no keeping this man happy. Some people just want to be angry. So, one day my dad came over and said if my mother didn't leave her ex, he would take my mom to court so he could take me to keep me safe.

I think that woke my mom up, because she never let the ex come back inside her apartment after that. And my dad was there to protect her in case he tried to stop by. My mother says her mother's courage also gave her courage. My mom says her mother was hit once, and she walked away from the relationship. This gave my mother strength in her darkest hour as she was remembering all the times she had been beaten by her ex. It was time to stop the cycle of abuse. And my dad and I helped her break that cycle, along with me, my apostle, and Jesus.

We are a family of faith. We have to be. It's times like these that challenge us and make us stronger. I used to ask my mom and dad why all this was happening. Why was I so sick?. Why was I beaten? Why did I have to have so many surgeries? And my mother would always say, "You are in God's hands. He made you special. You are a child of faith, and because of you, others will learn how strong they can be when life gets hard." Even though we still have our challenges, and my parents have to remind me why things like this happen, I'm so blessed to have my family. My real dad helps take care of us now: me, my mom, and my baby sister, Le Le. We are so happy, and not a day goes by that I don't pray for my entire family and give thanks to God for giving me such a good family.

Medical Challenges

I already told you that I have a lot of medical conditions. You probably thought, "OK, she has a heart condition and a leaky valve." But it's way more than that. I am listing everything here, not to make you feel bad for me. I am including this list in my book to show you that even with all these conditions, I still have a good life. I'm still here.

Some days are challenging, but sometimes you have to fight for what you want. And I do that every day by praying to God and asking my family for what I need, like if I need medicine or to go to the doctor. And I want you to be here, too. So, maybe this list will give you courage and make you feel less alone if you have a lot going on too.

Chapter 2

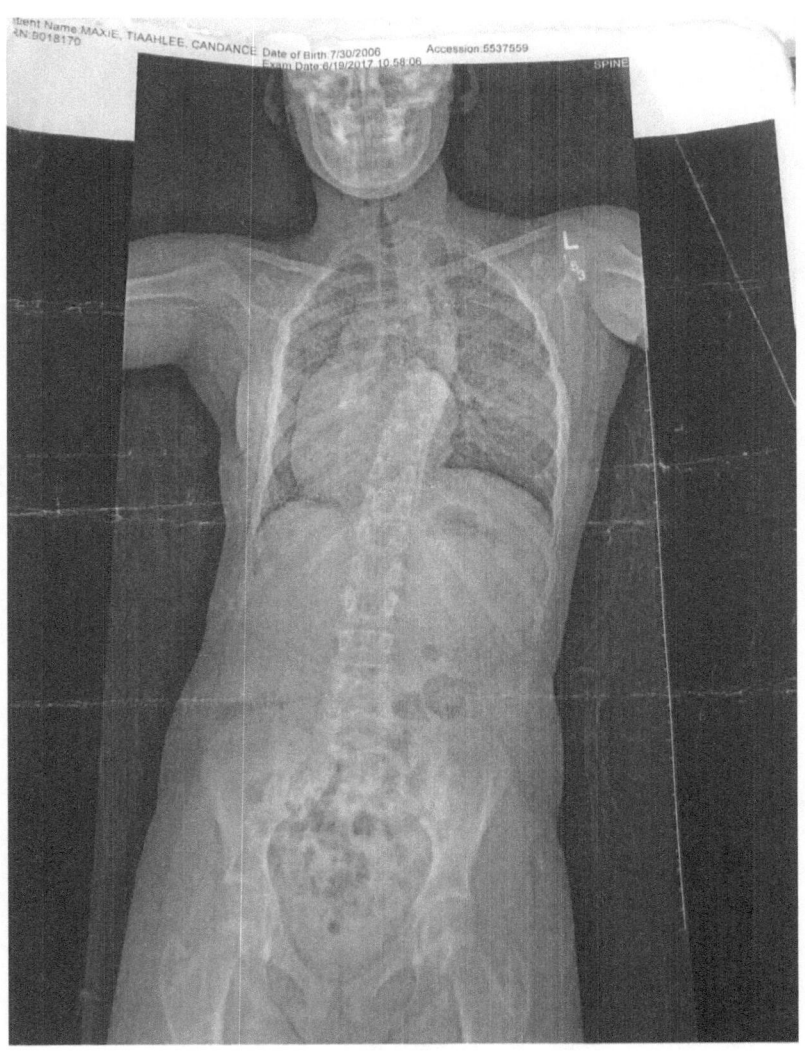

This is an X-ray of what my insides look like.
There's a lot of stuff happening in my body.

A Child of Faith

Here's the list of all my medical conditions:

1. Acute respiratory failure
2. Asthma
3. Atrioventricular septal defect
4. Cataracts (in both eyes; my doctor says I may be blind when I am twenty-four)
5. Collateral circulation
6. Complete atrioventricular canal defect
7. Cyanosis
8. Dextrocardia
9. Double outlet right ventricle
10. Essential hypertension
11. Fluid overload
12. Heart failure
13. Heterotaxy syndrome
14. Left atrial isomerism
15. Major aortopulmonary collateral artery
16. Mirror-image arterial arrangement with situs inversus
17. Pulmonary atresia
18. Retinal anomaly

Chapter 2

19. Secondary scoliosis
20. S/P bidirectional Glenn shunt
21. Sleep apnea
22. Supraventricular tachycardia
23. Unspecified pleural effusion
24. Hypermobility

I'm also on several medications to help me feel better. It's a lot, but I'm used to it now. Some of them I take daily. Others are for when I have an infection and need more medicine.

1. Acetaminophen-codeine
2. Adcirca
3. AeroChamber Plus Flo-Vu w/mask
4. Ambrisentan
5. Amoxicillin
6. Aspirin
7. Azithromycin
8. Bacitracin
9. Brompheniramine-pseudoephedrine-DM
10. Carvedilol

A Child of Faith

11. Cetirizine
12. Cyclobenzaprine
13. Depo-Provera
14. Docusate
15. Dulera
16. Enalapril
17. Ergocalciferol
18. Esomeprazole
19. Fluticasone
20. Furosemide
21. Gabapentin
22. Ibuprofen
23. Iron
24. Kristalose
25. Levalbuterol
26. Loratadine
27. Medroxyprogesterone
28. Melatonin
29. Methocarbamol
30. Montelukast
31. Norethindrone
32. Nortriptyline
33. Nystatin
34. One-A-Day Teen Advantage/Her tabs
35. Oxygen-helium inhalation
36. Pantoprazole
37. Polyethylene glycol
38. Sodium chloride (nasal solution)
39. Spacer/Aero-Hold chamber mask
40. Tranexamic acid
41. Trazadone
42. Vanatab DM
43. Vitamin D3
44. Wheelchair (not really a medication, but I still need it)
45. Prayer (the best medicine of all; use daily)

Chapter 2

Sounds like a lot, and it is. But if it helps me, then I need to take it.

Since I was a baby, I have had many emergency surgeries, including fifteen BT shunts and four open-heart surgeries. Because I have so many pulmonary veins reaching out to help me breathe, the doctors say it isn't safe to operate now because I could bleed out. I have to pray that I will not need any more surgeries.

During my first year of life, I had lots of medical treatment. You already know about the BT shunt I got when I was just four days old. It was put in to do the work of the pulmonary artery I was missing. But then I had three other emergency procedures because I started having issues with the shunts they put in. When one shunt stopped working, they'd add another. I also couldn't digest any food still, so I had to stay on PediaSure. And when I was six months old, I flatlined because I was not getting oxygen.

When I flatlined at six months, my parents had to rush me to the hospital where we live. When it happened, I started coughing and wheezing real loud. My parents ran into my bedroom and started giving me oxygen and told me everything was going to be OK, even though inside, they were very scared. My mom says it was a very bumpy ride to the hospital because my dad was speeding over the railroad tracks to get me there in time. They were very worried about me, and my mom kept looking back at me while my dad was driving.

A Child of Faith

One time my mom looked back, she said I was smiling and reaching my arms toward the sky. I wasn't crying; I saw Jesus and my angels. My mother asked Pat, "Why is she smiling? Can you see that?"

My dad looked in the rearview mirror and saw me reaching up toward the ceiling of the car. He nodded because he was driving and couldn't look for very long. "Maybe she sees something."

My mom started to cry, "Please don't take my baby. Please, Lord, let her be OK."

My baby photo under angel wings. Jesus and the angels always protect me.

Chapter 2

While my parents were driving, Jesus and my angels comforted me with their love because I was very scared when I couldn't breathe. Jesus and my angels played with me to keep me happy. That's why I was smiling. I knew I was going to be OK because I felt so loved and comforted.

When we got to the hospital, my parents were freaking out. I don't remember any of that. Just the part about Jesus and my angels. My mom says they gave me CPR and a whole lot of oxygen and put an IV in to help me get some fluids. There were eight people in the tiny room. They asked my parents to back up so they could work on me. It was hard for them to leave because they wanted to make sure I was OK, but they had to trust that the doctors would take good care of me.

While the medical team was working on me, my mom called Texas Children's Hospital to let them know what was happening. They said it sounded like I wasn't getting enough oxygen to my brain. My mom told them I also couldn't eat and was still on PediaSure, and she wanted to know why that was happening. They scheduled an appointment for me to see my doctor the following week to address my mom's concerns. When we got there, I was admitted, and they did a heart cath the very next day. They told my mom I needed more procedures done, but my mom couldn't stay for them to do everything that day, so they changed around some of my medications to keep my heart beating until we could come back.

When we returned, the social worker helped my mom find

A Child of Faith

a place to stay in the Ronald McDonald House so she could be with me for the week. While we were there, my doctor put in a bidirectional Glenn shunt to allow my blood to flow evenly between my vena cava and the new BT shunt they created to function as my pulmonary artery because the old one was not working well. The doctor said I needed a wider shunt because I had grown since the one they put in when I was first born. The new shunt had several branches like a tree so I could receive as much oxygen as possible. My mother says it looks like a hand reaching up to God. I like that, and I think she's right, because God is always ready to help me.

They told my parents that my baseline oxygen was right at 60 percent. They said to monitor it, and if it gets lower than that, it can be dangerous, and I need to see a doctor right away. They also let my mom know that my heart, lungs, and blood vessels are flipped. So, you know how when you do the Pledge of Allegiance at school and put your right hand over your heart? I have to put my left hand over my heart because my heart is on the right side of my chest instead of the left. At first, my teachers thought I was being silly or disrespectful and would come and tell me to change hands. But when my nurse explained that I was born with my heart on the other side of the chest, they understood that I wanted to participate. My heart was just in a different spot.

Sometimes you just need to educate people when you are different so they can understand you better. Try not to take

Chapter 2

it personally when they don't get you at first. They just don't understand you yet. But each time you share something about yourself, they get to learn about you more and more. Just be brave, and if you aren't ready, have an adult explain for you. Your teachers should always know if you have a special condition or need additional accommodations. That way, if they see other students teasing you or being mean to you, they can tell them to stop and try to help them understand you better.

By now, you know I was born with a lot of medical conditions. Maybe you were too. If so, you are probably on lots of different medications like me, and maybe you even need oxygen to breathe. If you do, please use it. It is there for you to help you breathe. The same goes for your medications. Please take them. Even if they taste bad or make you feel bad for a little bit after. Mine always help me feel better. Even the ones I don't like taking.

And this is something I want those of you who may be suffering to know: God is always with you. No matter what is happening to you or what is going on around you, just have faith and don't think about negative things. Think about fun things that you like doing with friends and family, and know that God will bring you through it. Keep telling yourself that everything will be OK. Because everything *is* going to be OK because God is always with you.

The power of Christ is what saved me and my mom. It's also what keeps us strong today. I encourage you and your family

A Child of Faith

to always pray before any surgery. Prayer always works and strengthens your faith. Prayer will also give you the courage to go through trying times, and give your family and loved ones peace while they are waiting for you when you are in surgery or at the doctor's office. Have faith and be strong because God is with you. Also, be nice to the doctor and your medical team. And ask them to pray, too. Prayer is good medicine. That's why it's on my list.

Chapter 3

I Will Boast All the More Gladly

Grandma Dolpha loves to sing.
She likes to hug me, too.
She's one of my guardian angels.
And I bet you have one, too.

—Tia'Ahlee Maxie

After I was born, my dad visited us every weekend. He was working three jobs (and still does) so he could help with our daily expenses. If my mom works, my sister and I lose Medicaid, and my mother cannot afford that since I need continued care and cannot be without coverage. My dad is really a good person. He knows I don't like riding in ambulances because they make me scared and increase my heart rate, which isn't good.

A Child of Faith

So he and my mom always drive me to the hospital, and they always beat the ambulance. They would do anything for me and my sister. That's just the kind of people they are. I am grateful that I was raised by such good people who taught me how to pray and ask God for help whenever I need it. Right now, I'm praying that my mom and daddy can get married. When I turn eighteen, the state will allow it without taking away my or my sister's insurance. I will be of age and can apply for my own insurance.

My dad visits as often as he can, and we are always happier when we are together. My sister, Le Le, and I always give him the biggest hugs when we see him. My mom's happier when he is around too. Soon, he'll be here all the time, and we can't wait for that day to come!

My dad has been there for me through many tough situations, and he has helped me and my mother through them. One of them was when I was just a baby, and I was in the hospital on Valentine's Day. I was having a lot of trouble breathing, and they put me on a ventilator. I had an emergency open-heart surgery. We had been at the hospital for two whole weeks so the doctors could monitor me to make sure I wasn't having any complications. They told my parents that if I didn't start breathing on my own, I would have more serious issues on top of what I was already going through.

While my mother was waiting, she kept praying that I would be able to breathe on my own. My dad says she asked

Chapter 3

This is my family. My dad, my mom, and my sister, Le Le.

that to be her Valentine's Day gift. She said, "Dear Lord, I don't want any candy. I don't want any toys. Please just help my baby get better." A tear rolled down my mother's cheek. And that's when my daddy wiped her tear and said, "Let's go buy her a gift. Talk positive, not negative. Let's look for something red. Your mother loved the color red." So my mom went with my daddy to the gift shop in the hospital. My mom still wasn't sure his plan was going to work, but she went with him anyway.

Well, as soon as they walked in, there was this red stuffed

animal, a frog, staring right at my mother! She picked it up, and it sang, "Let me call you sweetheart. I'm in love with you . . ." When my mom saw the frog, she lit up. Maybe it was a sign that I would be OK.

When my parents went back to the ICU, they asked if they could see me. The nurse waved them in, and I was breathing on my own! They had just taken me off the ventilator, and my mother and father were so happy. The prayers and positive thinking worked!

Mom, Dad, and me when I was little

Chapter 3

My mother asked if she could hold me. When I was on the ventilator, there was too much stuff in the way, but now, after two weeks, she was finally able to take me into her arms and hold me close. She was so happy she began to cry, saying, "Praise God. Praise Jesus," over and over. My dad was right there with her, holding my tiny little hands and kissing my forehead, relieved that his baby girl was going to be OK.

It was a happy day when my parents were able to bring me home. My mother says I played with that frog over and over. She says that frog got on her nerves sometimes, but it also helped me get off the ventilator, so she was patient with me and listened to my frog sing to me for hours on end. When it was bedtime, though, she put it away because we both needed some sleep. But when it was morning, I reached for my drawer where my mom had put the frog, and we started all over again with the singing frog: "Let me call you sweetheart . . ."

Meeting Grandma Dolpha

One time, when I was three, my parents were driving me to a doctor's visit. My mom says I kept calling my grandma's name, "Dolpha! Dolpha! Dolpha!" over and over again. My mom was confused and looked first at Daddy and then at me. I was reaching up for my grandma toward the sky, smiling. I could see her like she was really there! My mom thought, no, I couldn't be calling her mother. She had passed some time ago.

A Child of Faith

Then I said her name again while reaching up for her: "Dolpha! Dolpha! Dolpha! Dolpha!" I was so happy I was giggling. Grandma Dolpha loves me so much and was tickling me. At that point, my mom knew it wasn't a mistake. I was calling out for her mother, only she had never told me her mother's name. This made my mom start to cry, because her mother had passed before I got to know her. Later, she told me she wished I had gotten to meet my grandma.

My mother asked me, "Is your grandma here, baby?"

And I giggled. I was so happy my mom could see her, too. But my mom didn't see her. She just asked if that's what I was looking at. I told my mother that Grandma Dolpha was one of my guardian angels who comforted me whenever I got scared.

My mom looked right at me and said, "How do you know her name?"

"'Cause she told me."

My parents looked at each other for a minute, and then my mom started to cry harder. I told my mom not to cry. That Grandma Dolpha was here for her, too, and that she wanted my mom to know she was proud of her for being such a good mother. I told my parents that she visited me a lot and that she loved us very much.

"How many times do you see her?" Mom asked.

"She's my angel, Mom. She comes whenever I need her."

My mother kept looking at me. I think she was trying to understand why I was seeing angels. But some things just can't

Chapter 3

be explained. And then I said, "It's OK, Mom. She watches you, too."

My mother dabbed her eyes. She was trying not to cry, but she was so moved that her mother was there right when she needed her the most. My mother was scared. So much was unknown. She was so stressed that it was hard for her to keep going some days. My mom said I saved her that day and that Grandma Dolpha did too.

・・・

After the first time my mother saw me reaching for Grandma Dolpha, she started to watch me closely to see if her mother was in the room with me or if I was reaching up for her. I think part of my mom wanted to talk to her mother. I told my mom to pray for Grandma Dolpha to visit, and one day, when my mom needed her the most, she came to comfort her, and my mom saw her just like I do!

That's how angels work.

I love God and going to church. It brings me so much comfort, just like my angels do. We go every Sunday, and I can't wait to see our pastor and apostle. They always give me a hug and ask how I am doing. I love them so much. I pray for them, just like they pray for me, because everyone needs prayer. It is the best medicine there is. I pray for my friends. I pray for my family. I even pray for strangers sometimes when my angels tell me to.

A Child of Faith

I love all my doctors. For example, my retina doctor who helps me with my eyes. He is so kind to me and my mother. I pray for him because I want good things to happen for him, too. I pray for all my other doctors, too. They are helping me to live a good life with my family, and they need prayer just like you and I do.

Whenever you are going through trying times, here is a prayer that may help you and others you know.

> *Dear God,*
>
> *Please watch over me.*
>
> *I am scared and going through a hard time.*
>
> *Please guide me and help me to do what is right.*
>
> *Send me the comfort and courage that I so desperately need.*
>
> *And watch over Jesus and all the angels and anyone who may need you now, too.*
>
> *In the name of the Father, the Son, and the Holy Spirit,*
>
> *Amen.*

Part 2

'Twas Grace That Taught My Heart to Fear

> And so it was with me, brothers and sisters. When I came to you, I did not come with eloquence or human wisdom as I proclaimed to you the testimony about God. For I resolved to know nothing while I was with you except Jesus Christ and him crucified. I came to you in weakness with great fear and trembling. My message and my preaching were not wise and persuasive words, but with a demonstration of the Spirit's power, so that your faith might not rest on human wisdom, but on God's power.
>
> —1 Corinthians 2:1–5, NIV

Chapter 4

When I Came to You

Not everyone is as they seem.
Some seem nice when really they're mean.
If you come across someone like this,
Tell your loved ones, tell your friends.
Being quiet helps no one,
No matter what they say.
And if they threaten or hurt you,
Tell someone right away.

—Tia'Ahlee Maxie

Ever since I was ten months old, my mother has hired a nurse to help take care of me. Because of my condition, I need round-the-clock care. At first, everything seemed OK with the new nurse. I don't remember much about her when I was a baby, but as I grew older, I started to notice she was mean.

The bad nurse was always nice to my mom but when my mom left to run errands or go to work, the nurse showed a different side to me. I guess she thought since I was little, she could take advantage of me. Or maybe because I was in a wheelchair and on oxygen, she could control me by keeping me away from my medicine when I needed it so I would give her what she wanted.

The bad nurse would come eight hours a day to give me my medication, check my vitals hourly, monitor me, and change my diapers when I was a baby. She became like family. For years she took care of me and even took me to daycare. My mother had cameras in the room. She told the nurse where they were because she trusted the nurse, which my mother regrets to this day.

When I was a baby, I remember crying in my crib, needing my diaper changed, and the bad nurse would turn up the volume on the TV and tell me to hush. When the nurse heard my mom's car pull up, she would give me my medication, put me on oxygen, and start to change my diaper, which had been dirty most of the day.

Then the nurse and my mom would talk, and they seemed to really like each other, so I didn't want to say anything bad about her because I wanted my mom to be happy. It seemed like they were becoming friends. A part of me wanted to scream out, "Mom, that's a bad nurse!" But I couldn't do it. I was afraid

Chapter 4

to because the bad nurse told me if I said anything, she would hurt me.

Good nurses won't tell you those kinds of things. So if you have a nurse that tells you that or something worse, please tell your family or the police. You deserve to be treated with love and respect, and if you aren't getting that from your nurse or doctor, your family needs to know so they can find you someone who can take better care of you.

From when I was ten months to eleven years of age, I never said anything to my parents. Partly because I was confused. The nurse was always so nice to my mother and my daddy. I thought maybe I was doing something wrong, and if I could make her happy as my mom did, then she would like me, too.

But nothing I did seemed to work. The nurse just got meaner and meaner the older I got. As soon as my mom left, the nurse was mean to me. When I was older, and my parents left for work, the bad nurse would tell me to clean up the house and to take my own medicine. She made me do chores like warm up her food. Pour her something to drink. Give her the remote. I felt like I was her nurse instead of the other way around. It was confusing because she was supposed to be taking care of me.

One day I was having chest pains and coughing up blood, and the mean nurse wanted me to get her a Coke. The nurse yelled at me and told me to hurry up. I couldn't walk because I was coughing so bad and felt weak. From my room, I heard her yell at me to be quiet because she couldn't hear her programs. If

A Child of Faith

I didn't shut up, she was going to walk in there and kill me. So I prayed for God to help me and found the strength to put on my oxygen. Eventually, the coughing got quieter, but I was having really bad chest pains. I told the nurse again that I was in bad pain, and she told me to hush. She said I had a heart condition and that was normal and to stop bothering her so much or she would show me real pain.

When my mom came home, I wanted to go give her a hug, but the nurse got to her first and hugged my mom. And when she left that day after hugging my mom and telling her what a good girl I was, she looked back at me with those mean eyes that said if I ever told my parents about her, she would kill me. Those eyes made me shiver. I can still see them today. Black as coal. Cold as ice.

Those were big words. She. Would. Kill. Me. She said that more than once because she knew what she was doing was bad, and she wanted me to keep quiet. And I did stay quiet because I was so afraid of her. I had been afraid of her since I was a toddler, and now, she was taking me to school.

I kept quiet even though I was being threatened by the very woman who was hired to take care of me. I was terrified that if I told my parents, the bad nurse would kill me, so we lived like that for many years.

I prayed to God, Jesus, and all my angels. They told me it would be OK. But there were some days that were really hard

Chapter 4

and nights that I cried myself to sleep because I felt trapped. I felt that I couldn't tell anyone.

But this was just the beginning. I had yet to learn what evil was waiting for me next.

Chapter 5

In Fear and Much Trembling

Through many dangers, toils and snares
I have already come,
'Tis grace has brought me safe thus far
And grace will lead me home.

—John Newton, "Amazing Grace"

The Bad Cousins

My mother has a welcoming heart. She is always wanting to help others, and I'm that way too. So I can understand why she took in two of my cousins when I was four years old. The boy was nine, and the girl was eleven. They were like a brother and sister to me. I was excited that I would have my cousins living with us. My mother took them in because they were living on the street in their mother's Suburban, and my mom wanted to give them a better life.

They lived with us for three years. Little did we know that life on the street had troubled them more than we could have ever imagined. Soon after they moved in, they started doing bad things to me in secret. They would tell me not to tell, or they would kill me. I was just a young girl, and it scared me when they would say that. So I would promise not to tell each time they took me into the bathroom to "play" with me.

I used to take baths with my older girl cousin. I didn't think anything of it. She was like my big sister, so I thought it was fun to have someone to play with in the tub. But one night, my parents went to the store and left her to watch me. My cousin put me in the bathtub like she always did, but then she locked the bathroom door and started to talk to me about "bad stuff" that I didn't understand. And then she kept touching my bottom. I didn't know why she was telling me these things or touching me like that. It made me scared, like something was wrong. I just didn't know what.

Then she put a towel on the floor, pushed me onto it, and got on top of me. She said we were going to make snow angels. I thought this was weird, because don't you make snow angels outside in the snow with lots of clothes on? But I didn't have a chance to ask my cousin that. Instead, she pushed me down on the towel and climbed on top of me while she was naked too. I started to scream, but my cousin put her hand over my mouth

Chapter 5

and told me no one would hear me, so I might as well stop screaming. Then my cousin said she would cut my other cousin if I didn't do what she said.

Another time, my female cousin made my male cousin do bad things to me during the night. One time, the male cousin told me he wanted to show me a "popsicle" and proceeded to put his private part in my mouth. It wasn't a popsicle. It wasn't cold. And it tasted awful. I tried to pull away, but he held my head down and said I had to keep sucking until whipped cream came out. I was crying because I didn't want to do this, and the female cousin pushed my head down and told me to be quiet. The other cousin said I would like the whipped cream in this popsicle and to keep sucking. Then he made a loud sound, and warm cream oozed into my mouth. But it was gross and tasted nasty. It didn't taste like Cool Whip, as he promised. I tried to spit it out, but he put his hand over my mouth and said, "Swallow it. Now!"

I knew if I didn't, he would hurt me, so I swallowed, and then they both laughed and left me alone in the bathroom. I cried so hard into a towel so no one would hear me. I was so ashamed and embarrassed and confused. I wanted to tell my parents, but my cousins said they would kill me if I did, so I felt stuck.

I didn't really understand what they were doing. I was just five, and they were older than me. Since they were like grown-ups, I thought I had to do whatever they said.

A Child of Faith

Another time, both of them brought me into the bathroom to make snow angels. I asked if I could get my coat and boots, and they laughed and locked the door. I told them I didn't want to take my clothes off, and the boy held my arms behind my back while my other cousin took off all my clothes.

Then they told me to lie back down and start making snow angels. So I did it, even though I didn't know why we were making snow angels inside again when it wasn't even cold outside. Then the girl cousin got on top of me like she did last time. She didn't have any clothes on either, and she started to kiss me on the mouth and touch me in bad places. I wanted to cry, but she put her hand over my mouth and did more bad things to me. Then my boy cousin told her it was his turn, and he did even worse things to me. He was heavy and breathing hard. His breath was hot, and he tried to kiss me on the mouth like my other cousin. I tried to get away, but he pushed down on me harder and put his tongue in my mouth. It was gross, and I didn't know why he would do that.

It didn't seem like something cousins would do. I never did that with my other cousins. This happened lots of times, and each time they warned me not to tell or they would kill me. When they did this, they would place both hands around my throat when they said it so I would understand.

One time my boy cousin asked me if I wanted to suck a lollipop. I told him I did because I liked lollipops, so he took me into the bathroom without his sister and locked the door. I

Chapter 5

knew something bad was about to happen. It always did when he locked the door after him. Then he gave me a creepy smile, unzipped his pants, and pointed down. He said he had a lollipop for me and pushed his penis right in my mouth, just like he did when he said he had a popsicle for me. It was gross. I coughed, and he hit me on the head and told me to be quiet and to keep sucking. Eventually, he made a sound, and he said it was special cream that he was giving me and that I needed to eat it.

It didn't taste like cream to me, but I ate it anyway. Before he left, he grabbed me by the throat, gave me a mean look, and said, "Remember what I told you. If you tell anyone, I will kill you." I nodded quickly. I was so scared of him and my other cousin. I kept quiet for a long, long time.

I was so confused. Why would my family hurt me and say they would kill me? I wanted to tell my mom and daddy, but I couldn't. So I kept the abuse a secret. I didn't even know what sexual abuse was or why I was crying so much. I felt like I must be bad for people to treat me like that. It made me feel alone and embarrassed. I felt so trapped, like I couldn't do anything about it because I was little.

I think they took advantage of me because of my heart condition, and they thought they could get away with hurting me like that because I was little, and they were older. They saw me as damaged and disabled. I was tired of being picked on. When I went to sleep at night, I prayed real hard that my cousins would stay away. I asked God and my angels to take them away. I felt bad asking God that, because they were family, but they were hurting me, and I didn't know what else to do.

This is when the angels started coming to me more and more. They gave me comfort and told me it would be OK. I had support from them, even though I was still afraid to tell my mom and daddy. Sometimes my cousins would come in my room and lock the door when my parents were at work, and it would start all over again with the snow angels and lollipops and new games that they came up with.

It was awkward at dinner, because they would give me mean looks when my parents weren't looking. I would just look down at my plate and pick at my food. I wasn't really that hungry, but my mom would encourage me to take a few more bites. It took me a long time to finish my supper, but I would eat as much as I could before going to bed.

One time, my mom told me to go brush my teeth before bed, and I just sat on the couch, afraid to move. She thought I was disobeying her, but really, I didn't want to go in the bathroom alone. But I didn't want to make her upset, so I brushed my teeth, and soon after, my cousins came and knocked on the door and said they wanted to brush their teeth too.

So I let them in, even though they really didn't want to brush their teeth. When they were done with me, I would sit in the bathroom and cry. I cried into a towel so my mom and daddy wouldn't hear me. I didn't want to be killed, so I was

Chapter 5

very careful whenever I did cry. When I cried, my angels would come in and wrap their wings around me and wipe away my tears. It made me feel better. I think that's how I lasted for as long as I did.

This went on for about three years. I was seven, it was almost Christmas (we had the tree up and everything), and we were all in the living room. My mother was talking about Christmas and how it was Jesus's birthday, and we would be celebrating soon. My mother noticed I was not happy, and she asked me what was wrong. I looked over at my cousins, and they gave me a real mean look. I knew what they meant without them even saying it.

My mom and daddy must have sensed something wasn't right. They asked me to come with them to their room and shut the door. I was scared. Were my cousins going to break down the door and kill me? Were they listening with their ears against the door? My heart was pounding in my chest, and I was fighting back three years' worth of tears.

My mom started: "Tia, baby, what's wrong?"

I shook my head and looked down.

Then my daddy bent down and gently lifted my chin.

"Did something happen to you?"

I kept looking down.

My parents must have known something wasn't right, and they told me it was OK. I was safe, and I could tell them.

"I can't tell you," I said quietly.

"Why?" Mom asked.

My daddy looked me right in the eye and said, "It's OK. We need you to tell us, Tia. We can't help you if we don't know what is going on."

I started to cry. I was so scared. If I told them, could they help me? What if they didn't believe me, and then my cousins came and killed me? I was not sure what to do. Then one of my angels came in and put her wings around me and whispered, "Tell them, Tia. It's OK."

Instantly, I felt safe, like it was OK to tell my parents what my cousins were doing to me. It took a lot of courage because I was still very scared and embarrassed. I thought somehow it was my fault.

But I told them while I was crying.

My parents were upset. My dad screamed and punched the wall. My mom bent down and hugged me.

"They need to go NOW!" my daddy said.

My mother wiped her tears. "I'm so sorry, baby girl. I'm so sorry. We didn't know."

I hugged my mom back. I was glad I finally told them.

My dad went out into the living room and whopped my cousins on the bottom hard and told them to pack their things.

"Get out of my house! Just get out!" he yelled as they ran to their room to pack.

My mom thought my dad was going to punch them, so she stepped in between them and said, "Go on, now, pack your things. It's time for you to leave."

Chapter 5

I could tell my daddy was mad. He smacked the wall and stared at my cousins as they went to their room to pack.

While they were packing, I was holding on to my daddy. I didn't want my cousins to try to kill me if my dad wasn't in the room. My mom called the police and my cousins' parents. When the police came, the bad cousins left with all their belongings. No one said goodbye. No one said they were sorry.

And as quickly as they came, they left. I was relieved but also scared. Would this happen again?

My dad asked if the police would press charges. They told him there was no case. The words I used to describe what happened, like "no no spots" and "coom coom," were too innocent. They said that it would be inadmissible in court.

Frustrated, my dad approached the father of the two cousins and told them what happened. Instead of being upset, my cousins' father actually laughed and said, "That's what young kids do. They play hide and go get."

My dad was so angry he wanted to beat the you-know-what out of their father, but my mom came and pulled them apart and said to come back inside. My daddy was so mad he didn't care if he went to jail. But my mom said, "No, Pat. Let's go inside."

I'd never seen my dad so angry before. Or my mother. That's when I knew how much they loved me and wanted to keep me safe. They told me if anyone does something to me that doesn't feel right to let them know or to call the police. No one should be allowed to harm another person. She has even told this to my younger sister, Le Le, so we are both prepared if we need to call for help.

After the police left, my mom was on the phone with Child Protective Services. Surely, they would help. But they dismissed the case too. They said there was no longer a threat since the cousins were gone. My mom hung up the phone. She couldn't believe what she was hearing. After she hung up, she took me to the ER to have me examined to see if I had been raped. I had bruises down there but no torn tissue.

At least they hadn't done that.

Chapter 6

I Was with You in Weakness

Jesus loves the little children,
All the children of the world;
Red and yellow, black and white,
They are precious in His sight,
Jesus loves the little children of the world.

—C. H. Woolston, "Jesus Loves the Little Children"

In Service of Others

I know we covered some heavy things in the last few chapters, so I want to give you a break from some of that and share some of the good things that have happened to me, too.

A Child of Faith

For example, ever since I was five years old, I knew I wanted to be a published author. I would make up stories in my head and started to write them down when I was a little older. I started drawing when I was about nine years old. And when I was ten, I wrote a few children's books. They are about a cat named Miffy. One is about Christmas, and another is about Halloween. And there is one about getting a new sibling, which can help kids who are getting a new brother or sister. I also wrote some books to help kids who are afraid of things like going to the dentist or going to the doctor. My dentist is the one who asked me to write the one about going to the dentist. A lot of kids (and grownups, too!) are afraid of going to the dentist. I hope my Miffy books get published one day, too, so I can help even more people.

Despite all the bad things that have happened to me, I want to help others. Friends, family, and even strangers, because we are all God's children, and Jesus wants us to be kind to others. I try to do that every day. I prayed to God about what I should do, and He said to share my story with others and encourage them to be good. God said He chose me to go through everything that is happening because He knows that I am strong enough to handle it. When He told me this, I understood I was supposed to help others who may be going through other things like this and that I could help them have faith when they read my book because they will see that I have faith, even when really bad things happen.

Chapter 6

Me and my sister, Le Le. We love each other so much.

A Child of Faith

Without faith, you lose hope. And God doesn't want you to lose hope. One way to increase your faith in God is to pray and help others. When you help others, you also help yourself, because it feels good to give and be there for other people who need your help.

My mother tells me I have a generous heart. When I tell her she gave me a good heart, she smiles. My sister has a good heart, and so does my daddy. We are so blessed to be together as a family, and I thank God every day for what we have and all the gifts that He blesses us with.

I truly believe that my apostle and pastor are in our lives to provide us comfort and guidance when we need it and also to bring us that much closer to God here on Earth. I also have my angels who are with me and bring me close to God and Jesus, including Grandma Dolpha, because she is one of my guardian angels.

When I was nine years old, I had a long meeting with God and Jesus that happened when I fell in PE class. You probably remember the bad nurse I was talking about earlier. Well, she was still my nurse when I was nine, and it seemed she got meaner every year. Sometimes I would wonder, why is she even a nurse? Aren't nurses supposed to be nice and help people?

Well, one day in PE class at my elementary school, my PE teacher said the whole class was in trouble for acting out and that we were going to have to run ten laps around the track. I wasn't one of the people who was acting out, and I couldn't run

Chapter 6

anyway because I used a wheelchair to prevent me from walking too much and losing my breath. So I didn't even go toward the track.

Instead, I asked my nurse if I could go to the playground, and she said, "No." She said I was going to have to do more work around the house when we got home because I was being bad. And if I didn't do what she said, she said she would tell my mother that I acted out in school.

All this time, the PE coach was screaming and came over and asked why I wasn't running. He yelled so loud that I pulled back. He asked why I couldn't run like the others, and I kept quiet. He scared me, and I just sort of froze there, not sure what to say.

Then he yelled, "You got to get up and run like everyone else because it's not fair that you just get to sit here while the others are working hard."

Rather than defending me and explaining to the coach why I couldn't run, the bad nurse told me to get up and run like everyone else. She said it wasn't fair that I was just sitting there watching everyone else run. I didn't look at her because I knew if I waited, she would hit me. Whenever no one was around, she would beat me with a closed fist if I didn't do what she wanted, like get her some Coke to drink or change the channel on the TV. I was scared to tell my parents what was going on because she said if I told them, she would hurt me. I asked what she meant. She didn't answer me. She just gave me a mean look that made me shiver.

A Child of Faith

She pushed me out of the wheelchair that day and smacked me hard on the bottom. "Go on, now. Run like the others!" Tears were streaming down my face. I knew I wasn't supposed to run. So first, I started walking, and the nurse told me to speed up. And then my friend Sissy came up to me and said, "Tia, Tia, why are you running? Why are you on the track?"

I was crying and said, "The coach and my nurse told me to run around the track. The coach said to run like everyone else, so I had to start running."

Then Sissy said, "That's not true. Tia, why didn't your nurse tell him? You're not supposed to be out there. Please tell me what's going on. I'll tell the teacher for you." Sissy looked over at the mean nurse, and I got scared. "Please, Tia. I can tell the teacher. Then he won't make you run."

I was terrified. Sissy didn't know how mean that nurse really was. I don't know if Sissy ever saw the mean looks she gave me. But I didn't want to get punched or hurt, so I shook my head and said, "No."

The coach noticed I was stopped and talking to Sissy, and he yelled at us to run. So I started running, maybe a hundred feet. I kept trying to run some more, and then I felt dizzy and saw white spots. My head was hurting so bad, and my heart was racing.

Sissy ran up and told me to sit down. "Why are your lips purple? Your fingers are purple, Tia. Your face is blue. Go sit down."

I knew I had to keep running, or the mean nurse would hurt

Chapter 6

me after I got home. So I kept trying to run, and that is when I fell. It was hot outside. I was lying on the ground. Then I saw my friends running to me, and my eyes closed.

Meeting Jesus

I didn't know this at the time, but I had flatlined. That's when your heart stops beating, and your brain waves stop. But not everyone who flatlines dies. Some come back when it isn't their time. This was the second time in my life this had happened to me. The first time I was a baby, just six months old. I just remember being comforted and feeling safe with my angels when I was younger.

Just like last time, there were two guardian angels to welcome me. But this time, I saw more. Much more. The angels placed their giant wings around me, and I knew I was almost in Heaven. At first, I saw a super tall gate that was shiny gold with sparkles. It looked like a billionaire's house. It was so beautiful.

The giant gates opened for me as I got close. When the gates opened, the light was really bright, with gold rays coming out. Then, through all the bright light, I saw Jesus and God. I also saw two more angels with giant gold wings guarding the gate. One of the angels held a tall staff, while the other had a bow and arrow. The one with the staff smiled at me, while the other one looked more serious.

I think they were archangels protecting the gates. They

nodded at me, and I stepped on a step when I first got through the gate. I noticed there were only two steps that I had to climb, but it looked like there were more steps that went up really high. When I walked into the Kingdom of Heaven, it was so shiny and sparkly. The whole place was gold. Gold floors, gold everything. On the wall behind God and Jesus, I saw this big sign that said, "God's Kingdom." And above God and Jesus's heads, there were all these different-colored flowers.

As my angels walked me closer, I got a better look at Jesus and God, who were sitting on giant golden thrones. I mean, these thrones were really big. Like eight feet tall and very wide. There was also a man sitting with them. Jesus and God were my color, and the other man was a darker brown than me. God had gray hair. It was real curly and smooth. The other man had a gray beard. This man was wearing a white robe and had a staff. He also had those wide gold bracelets on his wrists, the kind that Wonder Woman wears. Then I looked over at Jesus. He had braids. They looked like locks, but they were smooth like my braids. Jesus had a white robe on. I remember He had holes in the middle of His hands and two more holes, one in the front of each foot, like from the crucifixion. But I knew He could stand, even with the holes in His hands and feet.

It was so peaceful there. I felt safe. I was actually excited to be in Heaven. The energy in Heaven is warm and feels really good. At first, I was hurting and had a chill when I got there,

Chapter 6

but all that pain went away as soon as I walked through those tall gates. When you are in Heaven, you are perfect. You don't feel tired or hungry or cold or anything bad.

As I kept walking, I noticed I could breathe. I mean, really breathe. I wasn't coughing. I didn't need to take oxygen or cough drops. I didn't need any medicine or a wheelchair to get around. I could walk as fast or as far as I wanted. And I could see. I mean, I could see *everything*. I didn't have to wear glasses. It's like I was perfect! Everything was perfect there!

I remember God had this powerful voice. It was very deep. And there was this long line of people waiting. Pretty soon, I was next in line. I remember I went to the front of the line very quickly. The people in front of me had died, and I heard them. Some went to Hell, and I had to cover my ears. The screams were so bad. And some went up to Heaven. For the good people that went to Heaven, I heard these chimes; they sounded like crystal wind chimes. And just like I had two angels with me, there were other angels showing the other people around. They would hold their hands, and when God and Jesus said it was OK, they would ascend quickly. I watched as a woman and a lady went up to the next level of Heaven. I was amazed at how fast they just disappeared.

Then I saw this man. He was real angry. He was disrespecting and fighting with God. I didn't want to watch, but I think God wanted me to see what was going to happen, so I peeked through my hands. Two other angels, who looked different from the ones that took the other people to Heaven, dragged the angry man, who was kicking and screaming bad things at God, and took him to Hell when this big black hole opened up. As soon as they left, I heard more screams from Hell, and then the hole closed up.

Then God was talking to me and welcomed me there. Jesus did too. I remember I was thinking, *Am I going to die?* And God said, "It's not your time yet. But we want to show you something." And then Jesus came up to me and said, "Tia'Ahlee."

He said my whole name. I was shocked. He knew my name. Just like that. I didn't have to tell Him. He just knew! And God knew what I was thinking before I said anything!

Then Jesus said, "Welcome to Heaven. I want to show you around. But before I do, I want you to know something. You are going to live a long time. This isn't your time, Tia. So you don't need to be afraid. You are a chosen one. I know you've been through a lot already, and you are going to go through a lot more bad things."

Even though Jesus was giving me good news, some of it was not so good. I didn't want to go through more bad things, but I knew Jesus would help me. He could see that I was a little worried about the bad things, and that's when He said, "You will handle it. You are strong. And I will always be with you. When you go back home, tell others to get closer to God." By the way He was saying it, I could tell He meant me, too. Then He

Chapter 6

looked closely at me and added, "Tell them that if they don't, they're going to end up in a bad, bad place."

I nodded. I would do just what Jesus said. Jesus then said, "And, Tia, my strong-willed prophetic bird, when it is your time, you will be back here. But that is a long way away. So please don't worry about that now. All you must do is stay close to me and share your story with the world. It's only if you are not good that you will end up in the bad place, like the others you just saw."

Jesus saw that I was scared, and then He knelt beside me. "I don't mean to scare you, Tia. I just want you to know what is true. I know you have a very kind heart. Keep it kind and give to others, and all will be well. I promise." That made me feel better, because Jesus always keeps His promises. Then He stood up and extended His hand. "It's OK. I will protect you."

I took His hand and smiled back at Him. He had the most loving smile, just like my mom and Grandma Dolpha. We sat on a rock, and He started to tell me about some things my mom was going through. Grown things that I shouldn't know about, but Jesus wanted me to know so I could pray for her.

I nodded and held His hand as I prayed. You know what else? I didn't feel the holes in His hands. After we finished praying, we were walking, and I was wondering where the holes had gone. Maybe they closed up when He held hands with people.

Jesus said, "Love cures all," and showed me His hands with no holes in them.

And I was like, "You heard that?"

Jesus smiled. "Of course, Tia. I hear everything. Just as my Father does."

Once He told me that, I didn't really need to talk, because Jesus would know what I was thinking. But sometimes I was so excited I couldn't help it, and words came out.

Then I saw another man who tried to fight the guardian who was taking him to Hell. The guardian was eight feet tall. He wore these gold metal boots and the same gold metal Wonder Woman bracelets. His suit was like gold armor that showed his muscles.

After the other man was taken to Hell, Jesus took my hand and said He wanted to show me the bad place. I was scared to hold His hand, and He said, "I'm not going to hurt your hand or let anything bad happen to you, Tia. I'm Jesus."

Even though I was scared, I trusted Jesus, and we went down into Hell. In Hell, there were these black coals on the floor, but they didn't burn my feet or Jesus's. That's when I knew I was really safe. Jesus was protecting me. I bet the coals burn other people real bad. But nothing bad was going to happen to me, even though it was really awful down there.

In Hell, there is a gate, too. But this gate is black, stinky, rusty, and red. And it has these sharp pointy tips that look like they would cut you bad if you touched them. When we walked through the gate, I didn't want to look at the Devil, because he was scary. He had a giant throne too, but it was dark and ugly.

Chapter 6

And there were two minions sitting next to him, one on each side of the Devil. Their thrones were rusty and smaller. I looked real fast and saw a sign that said, "The Devil's Kingdom." Even though I was scared, I remember feeling so smart because I was only five, and I wondered, *How can I read this?* When I flatlined, I was really nine, but it's like we went back in time, and I was five years old again when I was in Heaven.

Jesus tugged gently on my arm to take me far away from Satan, who was looking at me and making creepy sounds. Even though Jesus was walking with me, Hell was really scary, and I didn't like it there. At first, I felt cold, and I was afraid something was going to come and grab me and eat me like in the scary movies. Then Jesus took me to this big cliff, and people were falling over the cliffs and yelling, "Please forgive me! Please forgive me! I'm sorry!"

But if they didn't jump, a big black hand pushed them over the cliffs, and the screaming grew louder. As they were falling, I heard more screaming in the pit and sounds like something was burning on a giant fire. And I heard people shout, "It burns! It burns! Aargh!"

While holding Jesus's hand, I peeked over the cliff, and it was like this junkyard with old, messed-up cars. It was burning. The flames were high. And I heard the Devil laughing whenever they screamed. It was a creepy laugh. One that I will never forget. I didn't know what to do. Jesus had walked with me, and there were a lot of people suffering. And they

A Child of Faith

all bent down and kneeled when they saw Jesus and me and asked for forgiveness. Jesus didn't say anything. He kept talking to me while shaking His head at the people begging Him to take them back.

When I was in Heaven, it felt like a nice dream. But Hell was like the worst nightmare you could ever imagine. It woke me up from the nice dream I was having in Heaven. It was so hot in Hell. My skin was hot and burning. It felt like you were on a hot stove, cooking. I was ready to get out of there. It smelled really bad there, like dead people and poop and vomit. It's like we were in this filthy abandoned junkyard with a cliff and a giant pit of fire. It was a horrible smell. I wanted to leave and didn't know why we were still there.

And then Jesus said, "Tia, if my people do bad things, they will end up here. So don't do bad things. Ignore the Devil. Do what I tell you. If you and others do what I tell you to do, you will end up in Heaven with me. I love all of you so much, but if you don't do what I want you to do, you will get punished, and you will end up here. God is our Father. And if you make Him mad, you're going to end up in a bad place." Jesus looked deep into my eyes when He said, "Tia, promise me you will be a good girl. When you go back, tell the whole wide world to get closer to God, and it will be a better world."

I nodded and told Jesus I would keep my promise. And He gently squeezed my hand, and then we were back in Heaven. I was so relieved. I didn't want to stay in Hell.

Chapter 6

When we got back, Jesus asked me, "Do you want to walk around?"

I nodded eagerly. I couldn't wait to see more of God's Kingdom.

Jesus took me to a stream. The water was so pretty and sparkly. It looked like diamonds were in the water. It was perfectly clear. He picked up the water, even with the holes that were back in His hands. He picked it up and said, "Drink this, Tia. These waters are very healing. It will help you."

I was amazed that the water didn't go through the holes in His hands. They made a perfect cup for me to drink. The water tasted like Blue Raspberry Nehi. In Heaven, I think water tastes like your favorite drink, and it's cool and refreshing to have. I felt greedy, but I wanted more of the blue water;

Jesus offering water when I flatlined and went to heaven.

it was so sweet and so good. Jesus smiled, scooped some more water for me, and said, "You can have more. This water will help you when you are hurting or going through painful times, Tia. Drink all you want."

After drinking the sparkly water, Jesus asked me if I wanted to stay or go home now. Before I could answer, I looked up and saw a Pegasus flying through the air, and a white unicorn with a sparkly gold horn slowly approached me. As I was watching the unicorn, the Pegasus landed nearby. Both the unicorn and the Pegasus went to the water to drink. I was so happy watching them. I wanted to pet them and play with them, but they were so magical I was afraid that if I touched them, they might run away. I didn't want this moment to end. It was so special.

I looked around and saw lions and lambs walking side by side. One of the lions was playing with a lamb, and they were rolling around and being silly. They liked Heaven too. It was cute to watch. I asked Jesus if I could have a lion like that one day if I shared what I experienced in Heaven with others. Jesus smiled. That smile told me He would give me the boy lion with the big mane that I liked one day because He already knew I was going to be good and share what I learned.

I was having so much fun that I didn't realize it was getting late. I didn't know the sun set in Heaven, too, just like it does at home. Jesus knew it was time for me to make a decision, so He walked me back to the giant gate where God and the other man were sitting.

Chapter 6

I looked up at God, and He asked me, "Would you like to stay with us, Tia? Or would you like to go back home with your parents?"

It felt so peaceful in Heaven. Part of me was sad to be back at the gate, because I loved being in Heaven with Jesus and God and all the animals and the sparkling water. But I also wanted to be back with my parents, even if it meant I would be sick or have pain.

It was a hard decision for me to make because nothing bad can ever happen to you in Heaven. You don't have to worry about getting teased or bullied or sick or getting bitten by spiders or mosquitos or snakes or sharks, because they are in the bad place with the mean people. While I was thinking over God's question, I looked around; every beautiful animal was there. And the birds, they were so beautiful and sang so sweetly.

Even though the water is magical in Heaven, you don't have to drink it unless you want to. You are already strong and can live off the pure air that God provides you. On Earth, you have to feed your body with food and drink, but in Heaven, your Spirit is already full.

I finally had my answer. I looked right at God and said, "I want to go home."

God smiled, and then He said, "I love you, Tia. Remember everything you saw here, and tell others what you have learned. You are the chosen one. I have charged you with special work, and even though the challenges you face are great, I know you

A Child of Faith

are strong enough to handle them. You will inspire many people who are facing similar challenges. You will teach them to be strong, like you."

I thanked God and Jesus for the lessons they taught me that day and for reminding me to be good. When I turned to leave with my angels, God said, "One last thing, Tia. I was going to send you home regardless, because it isn't your time yet. So you answered wisely, just as I knew you would."

• • •

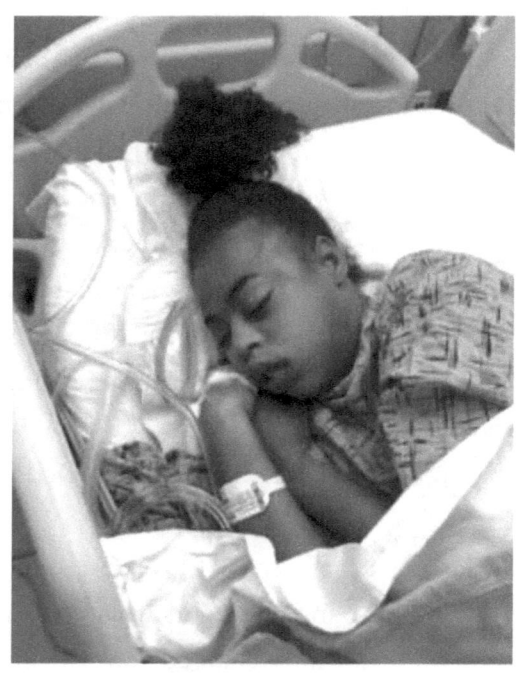

Me in the hospital after I flatlined

Chapter 6

When I woke up, I was in the hospital. There was a doctor looking over me, and I heard monitors beeping in the room. I looked down and saw an IV in my arm and the bad nurse in a chair off to the side.

The doctor said, "You're awake. Are you OK, Tia?"

I nodded, still trying to figure out what just happened.

Then she asked, "Do you remember what happened today?"

The doctor was nice. I felt safe when she was in the room. But the bad nurse gave me a mean look like I wasn't supposed to say anything. But I couldn't remember what there was to tell.

Then I turned back to the nice doctor and said, "I don't know. I just remember I went to sleep, and then I woke up and saw Jesus."

"Wait, what? What do you mean you saw Jesus?" The doctor seemed confused and a little worried.

"I don't remember what was going on before I saw Jesus" was all I could say.

When the doctor left, I asked the bad nurse why I was at the hospital.

"You just had a little scare. You must have passed out in PE class, and this is why you ended up here."

I was confused. "How did I pass out?"

The bad nurse looked down and fidgeted with her bag. "That's what we don't know. Some sort of accident."

I knew she was lying by the way she said it and how she

couldn't look at me when she talked, but I didn't dare say that to her.

"If I'm in the hospital, where are my parents? I want them here with me."

The bad nurse had an answer for everything. She raised her head and said, "Your mom already came, but she couldn't stay long. Your daddy stayed for a while with you too, but you were asleep. He had to go to work too. Don't worry, they were here with you."

When the doctor gave me the OK to go home, the bad nurse helped me out of bed after the hospital nurse removed my IV and EKG pads. Why do those pads always hurt coming off and leave all that sticky goo? I wished they could listen to my heart another way. But finally, they were off, and I could go home.

The bad nurse and I got home late that night. Before we went into the house, she grabbed my arm and squeezed it hard. "You say one thing to your mom and daddy about what happened today, and I will kill you. You hear me, child? They been through enough today. No need to add more to their stress. I do so much for you as it is. We don't want to worry them any further."

"But they know, right?" I asked, ducking to avoid her familiar slap.

"Course they know. I just don't want you to keep bringing it up. Now we're going to tell them you had to stay late

Chapter 6

today, is all. And that is all we are going to say. Tell me that you understand."

The bad nurse wouldn't let go of my arm until I nodded. It didn't make sense. If they knew, wouldn't they want to stay late with me? Tears were running down my cheek. She was hurting me, but I couldn't say that, or she would punch me hard. So I wiped my tears and got out of the car, and the mean nurse put on her fake smile and rolled me into the house in my wheelchair.

When the nurse wheeled me inside, my mother came running over to me. "Tia, baby. Where have you been? I called Pat. He didn't know where you were. So I called the school, but they were closed. Why are you home so late?"

I froze. I knew I wasn't supposed to say anything, so I let the bad nurse comfort my mother. She placed an arm on my mother's shoulder and said, "I just took her out for ice cream after school so she could have a special treat. She did all her homework and was extra good today. Then we went to the Dollar Store, and I got her a little something after, just to cheer her up."

The nurse handed my mother a stuffed animal that she had purchased in the hospital gift shop. My mother was confused, but she seemed OK with things now.

"You sure you OK, baby? I called Pat, and he didn't know either. I've been worried sick about you."

My mom came over and hugged me. I nodded my head against her warm chest. She loved me big. It's like she could make all the bad go away. I didn't want my parents to worry. And I didn't want to be killed. So pretending and lying was all I could do right then to save my life. And theirs. I didn't trust the mean nurse around my parents either. That's how evil she was to me.

I know you aren't supposed to lie, but sometimes when it comes to survival, those kinds of lies are different. They are there to save you from bad people. You never have to tell bad people the truth. You can make them think you are playing their game, but all games, no matter how clever, always come to an end, whether the players want them to or not . . .

The Bad Nurse and The Good Mr. Moore

After meeting Jesus, I was back in class the next day like nothing had happened. For two years, I pretended that everything was OK until one of my teachers, Mr. Moore, asked if I was coming to recess that day. He wondered why I never came outside. But before I could answer, my nurse said, "No. She's staying in. We'll be outside later on."

He looked at her funny, like when you think someone might be lying to you. He said to the nurse (but really, he was talking to me), "Are you sure?"

The nurse glared at me, and I nodded obediently. I knew better than to say anything, and I had the welts on my back to prove it. But it was different this time. Mr. Moore saw how the nurse looked at me. He could tell I was afraid of her.

Chapter 6

"OK. I'll see you outside, Tia. Come on out when you're ready, OK?"

I kept still. I didn't nod. I didn't say one word. I knew if I did anything, I would be punched by the bad nurse.

After Mr. Moore closed the door, the bad nurse told me, "You don't deserve to be out there playing with the other kids. You need to do extra work." She opened up the math book to the part we hadn't done yet and said, "You have to do extra homework."

"But I can't do this yet. We're still learning the times tables."

Then the bad nurse made her big mistake. She yelled at me and pounded on the desk so hard I wondered why her fist didn't bleed.

"You stupid child! You do what I say."

I nodded and looked at the homework as tears dropped on the page.

Whack!

I winced at the slap on my cheek.

"Stop your crying, Tia! If you want to go to recess with the other kids, you better hurry up and do your work."

I wanted to go outside so bad. Why was she making me stay when everyone else got to go?

"But I don't know how to do this yet."

Then the nurse punched my back two times, hard.

"Ow!"

"That's what happens to stupid children."

I tried not to cry, but my face and back were screaming in pain.

I didn't know this, but Mr. Moore was listening right outside the door to the classroom. He heard everything.

I was crying. *Loud.* And then I said, "I want to go outside."

The nurse raised her hand like she was going to slap me and said, "Hush!"

While this was happening, another teacher in the hallway heard me crying in the classroom. Mr. Moore told her to call my mother. Then he grabbed another teacher as a witness. As soon as they walked in, they saw the bad nurse punch me *hard* in the back, and Mr. Moore yelled, "What are you doing? Why are you hurting this child?"

The mean nurse shot Mr. Moore a dirty look. I never saw Mr. Moore angry, but he looked real upset that day. Then he approached me, and I wasn't sure what he was going to do. I could tell he was angry at the bad nurse. But I wasn't sure if maybe I did something wrong, too, because I didn't finish my homework.

"Tia, is she supposed to do that? Does your mother know what she is doing to you?"

I kept quiet. I didn't want to get killed. The bad nurse said she would kill me if I told. But Mr. Moore kept asking questions.

"Does she have a right to hit you? Did your mother give her permission to beat you?"

I tried to hold it all inside, but it was like everything I had

Chapter 6

kept secret for all these years burst out of me like a flash flood filling the room with all my tears. I started crying. I didn't know what to say. I knew what the nurse was doing was wrong. But I was afraid to say anything because I believed her when she said she would kill me.

Mr. Moore stayed in there with me and yelled at the mean nurse: "You aren't supposed to hit other people's kids!" Another teacher was in there with Mr. Moore, and she lifted my shirt and saw all the marks on my back from all the beatings.

They were shocked. I could tell because they both gasped and made surprised faces.

While the teachers were talking, I kept crying. I was so scared that I was going to get in trouble at school, that the mean nurse would kill me, and that my mom would be very upset at me for not telling her that the nurse was bad.

But before my mom got there, the mean nurse hurried up, got her stuff, and left. After she left, Mr. Moore kept asking me questions: "Does your mom know about this? Tia, why didn't you tell me this was happening?"

I burst into tears again. I felt bad. I knew I should have told, but I was scared.

And then the courage came, and I said, "She said she would kill me if I told."

Mr. Moore was very upset when he heard this. He pointed to the welts on my back. "Are these all from her?"

Between sobs, I managed to say, "Yes, sir. I was afraid to

make mistakes on my homework, or she would beat me. She beat me for lots of things. I don't know why."

I felt safer, like I could tell him things now that the bad nurse was gone.

Mr. Moore sat in a chair next to me and said something I will never forget: "You shouldn't be afraid of anybody. Promise me you will not let anyone do this to you again. Tell me. Tell your teachers. Tell your parents. You are a good person and deserve to feel safe."

I nodded and wiped away as many tears as I could. And then my mom arrived.

"Where is she?!"

My mom was furious. She wanted to confront the nurse, but the bad nurse wasn't there. Then my mom came running into the classroom and gave me a big hug, and we both cried together for a while.

Mr. Moore gave us a moment. Then he approached us and said, "I heard the nurse say Tia was disobeying her and that she needed to be disciplined. That's when I went and got another teacher. We heard Tia crying, and we walked in and found her with the nurse. I'm so sorry, Ms. Calvin. I wish I had known sooner."

Between tears, my mother said, "You didn't know. It's not your fault." Then my mom gave Mr. Moore a hug. "Thank you for saving Tia."

Before we left the school, my mom stopped to talk to the lady in the front office.

Chapter 6

I could tell my mom was upset, because she didn't say hi or anything. She just blurted, "Did you know?"

The lady in the office looked down at the floor.

"You knew she was hurting my baby? Why didn't you tell me Tia's nurse was beating on her?"

The lady backed away and said, "I thought y'all were cool. I didn't want to upset you. I thought maybe you knew."

My mother shook her head. "No, ma'am. I did not know. Do you think I would want someone beating my child?"

The lady got real quiet. She didn't know what to say to that. So my mom shook her head and gave the lady one last look before she pushed me out of the office in my wheelchair and took me home.

"I'm so sorry. I'm so sorry," Mom kept saying while she was driving. She was crying, too, and wiping her eyes so she could see the road.

When we got home, my mother called the police, but they wouldn't do anything about it because the nurse wasn't in the house with us, so she wasn't considered a threat. Just like what they said about my mean cousins. While my mother was talking to the police, I got my courage back and told her about the time the nurse and I got home late when I was nine. It wasn't because she was buying me things. It was because I passed out in school and was in the hospital. I told her how the mean nurse made me run in PE. Then I saw fire in my mom's eyes when I told her that. I knew she was mad. Not at me for keeping the secret, but at the bad nurse for making me.

How could she not tell my parents that I had been in the hospital? Parents want to know if their children are hurt. As soon as I told her that, my mother called the school and learned what happened that day in PE. Then she called the agency where the nurse came from. Mom wanted to file criminal charges, but they couldn't press charges because they said they didn't have proof. But they did fire her. I hope she (or someone like her) is not with another child right now. If you are reading this and your nurse is being mean to you, please tell someone you trust. Everyone deserves to be safe. Do not believe their lies. Those lies are to control you and keep you scared. You do not need to be scared. You deserve to have a good nurse.

Nurse B.

After the bad nurse left, we had to find a new nurse to take care of me while I was in school. My mom and I interviewed a *lot* of people this time.

My mom had a few questions prepared to judge the character of the person who would be taking care of me, and Miss B. passed with flying colors. Not because she was perfect but because she was honest, and that's exactly what we wanted.

"Why do you want to be a nurse?" was the first question my mom asked.

And Miss B. said, "To be honest, I didn't. But I needed a job, and it was something I just did."

Chapter 6

Miss B. also looked at me and listened to what I needed from her. She didn't cut me off. It was like she wanted to hear what I had to say, which was very different from the other nurse.

Then my mom asked, "Why are you still a nurse?"

Miss B. said, "Because it pays well, and I actually like the work."

And that's all my mom needed to hear. She knew Miss B. was good people. When Mom told her about my medical conditions, Miss B. said she had scoliosis like me, so already we had something in common. (Although my scoliosis was because of the mean nurse who beat me in the back; Miss B. was born with hers.) My mother also knew Miss B.'s ex-husband, so it gave my mother a sense of comfort to know that she knew someone who knew our new nurse. It made Miss B. feel like less of a stranger to us.

When my mom met with Miss B. that first day, one of the first things she noticed was that she was nice and honest. I'm glad she passed Mom's test, because Miss B. was my nurse for six years. She treated me like one of her kids and bought me snacks and stuff. Sometimes we got on each other's nerves like she was my other mom. But that's cool. Because she was like family.

Miss B. sometimes encouraged me to get up out of my chair and make new friends. At first, I was like, "No, I don't want to go over there." So she'd nudge me and tell me, "I want you to have new friends, Tia. If I go up there with you, I'm going to look like a creeper. Go on. I know you can do it."

So I trusted her and got out of my wheelchair, walked over to the kids, and started talking. And it worked. I became friends with some of them because Miss B. gave me a little nudge, just like a mama bird pushes her baby bird out of the nest when it is time to fly.

My first "flight" went well because I made some new friends. I liked that about Miss B. She pushed me but in a good way, like she wanted me to succeed and to be happy. But she could also get real.

One time, I was struggling to breathe at school. I'm not gonna lie; I don't like to use my oxygen in class because I get teased when I use it. So, after I was coughing a bunch one time, Miss B. asked me if I wanted to go outside. That's what she would say whenever I needed to use my oxygen. It was like our secret code. And I nodded yes, because I was coughing so hard I couldn't speak.

Well, this one time, I needed my oxygen real bad, and I remember she pushed me through the hallway, and there were all these kids in the middle of the hallway. She screamed, "MOVE," but they kept talking, and not everyone got out of her way. So, using my wheelchair, she bumped into the ones that didn't and told the kids to move.

Miss B. didn't play when it came to my health. I knew she would do the same thing with me if she had to rush me to the hospital. She'd be talking to my mom on her cell while driving as fast as she could. And knowing Miss B., she'd just leave

Chapter 6

her car right out front of the ER because she wouldn't want to waste time trying to find a parking spot. She knew every second would count when it came to me, and she probably wouldn't care at that moment about her car. She would just want me to be OK. For many years I felt safe with Miss B.

Miss B. was a good nurse to me and my family, but over time she started to come later and later and was unable to keep to my early schedule. My mom let her come later, but that became a problem because she started arriving even later than she promised. She also seemed more distracted and was not able to provide the special care I needed while I was at school. My mom noticed I started getting moody, which was unlike me. She kept asking me what was going on, but I didn't want to say anything bad about Miss B.

I really believe Miss B. is a good person. I just think she was getting tired of being a nurse, because she wasn't taking very good care of me anymore and started talking more on her cell phone at school. I recently hurt my hand because she let the door hit me instead of wheeling me outside like she usually did. When my mom saw my swollen hand, she told me we were going to get a new nurse. While it was hard to say goodbye to Miss B. because she was like family and had taken good care of me for so many years, my mom told me sometimes people change, and if they turn on you, it's time to let them go. When you are like me and need a nurse to watch and take care of you, it's important to have one that will always be there for you.

A Child of Faith

If you have a nurse, be sure to tell your parents if they are taking good care of you. But if they start coming late or stop taking good care of you, let them know that, too. Your needs come first. That is why you have a nurse. And maybe you will have to get a new nurse from time to time like me. That is OK. What matters most is your health. And sometimes that means saying goodbye to someone you care about if they can no longer care for you.

Chapter 7

In Demonstration of the Spirit— Spending Time with Grandma Dolpha

Angels all around us—
Every single day.
Whenever you feel scared,
Just close your eyes and pray.
Angel wings are big and soft.
Their eyes shine ever bright.
They like to spend time with you—
Wings ready to take flight.

—Tia'Ahlee Maxie

When I was two years old, my mother took me to see a therapist because she kept finding me talking to someone whenever I was playing dolls or having tea parties. What she didn't realize is that I was talking to Grandma Dolpha.

When I was a baby, my mom heard me calling for Grandma Dolpha, but it had been a while since that happened. When we went to therapy, my mother asked if it was OK if I had imaginary friends at that age. I kept trying to tell her that I wasn't imagining anything, but my mother said we had to go see the doctor.

When she started telling the therapist what I was doing at home, I said: "Not imaginary, Mom. Real!"

The therapist chuckled and asked me, "So you have real friends, Tia?"

I nodded. "Yes, I have parties with my angels in my room every afternoon."

The therapist and my mother exchanged glances. My mom seemed worried, but the therapist just smiled.

"I think your daughter is perfectly fine, Ms. Calvin. It's completely normal to have friends like these at her age."

I tugged at my mother's sleeve. "Real, Mom. Real."

My mother looked down at me. Even though she smiled at me, I could see something wasn't right. Like she didn't really believe me.

"So you're saying it's normal for my child to have tea parties and Barbie playdates with other 'friends' in the room?"

I nodded and smiled big at my mom.

The therapist smiled too. "That's right. Now, if this persists, say beyond age four or five, please make another appointment.

Chapter 7

But from what I can see here, Tia is perfectly fine. You have nothing to worry about."

When we left, my mother asked me in the car, "Do you see anyone now?"

I shook my head.

"Well, do you want to stop at McDonald's and get a Happy Meal?"

I was excited. I loved the Happy Meal toys. Sometimes we would go in and sit down, and I would get to play on the playground, but I could tell she was worried about something, so we went through the drive-through this time.

"Two Happy Meals, please, and one caramel ice cream without peanuts."

My mom would always get a Happy Meal, too, so I could have two toys instead of just one. I didn't like the food in the Happy Meals, so she would order me a caramel ice cream to eat. After she paid for the food, I smiled all the way home and let my feet swing back and forth against the back of my mom's chair. I was so happy. I couldn't wait to see what toys we got this time.

After we ate, Mom let me open the toys: We got Nemo and Dory! I was so excited because I loved *Finding Nemo*. I watched it over and over. At first, I was nervous that Nemo got lost, but my mother would watch it with me and tell me it would be OK, and she was right. Nemo found his dad at the end and got to swim home with him and all his friends.

Playtime with Grandma Dolpha

When it was time for bed, my mom helped me brush my teeth and get into my PJs. She went into her room to get ready for bed, and I started playing with Grandma Dolpha. I think my mom heard me from her room and came out and watched me from the door. I was laughing and playing and holding Nemo up in the air like he was jumping out of the water, and Grandma Dolpha held Dory up so she could play with Nemo. We were having fun, and then I heard my mom start to cry.

"Mom, come in here! Grandma Dolpha and I are playing Finding Nemo. Watch!"

My mother watched as my grandma and I moved our fish through the imaginary sea. My mother couldn't see Grandma Dolpha, but she did see the other fish moving on its own in the pretend ocean in the air above the floor. Grandma Dolpha was good at playing Finding Nemo. She always helped Nemo find his way home.

"What's wrong, Mom?"

I noticed my mother was still crying. I looked over at Grandma Dolpha, and she told me to ask Mom to play.

"Do you want to play, Mom? Grandma Dolpha says she's tired."

My mother looked at me and the toys I was moving through the air, now with both of my hands. She sat down next to me on the floor and took Dory.

Chapter 7

"Is Grandma Dolpha who you've been playing with?"

"Yes, Mom. I told you she likes to play with me. She also visits if I'm sad or scared."

My mom stroked my hair and gave me a hug as she wiped a tear on her cheek. "Time for bed, baby girl. We can play some more tomorrow. OK?"

I gave Mom a big hug and fell asleep dreaming of Nemo and Dory and all their friends in the great big ocean. The sound of the waves and Nemo and Dory swimming in the water took me into a deep and happy sleep.

Other Angels

It wasn't just Grandma Dolpha who would visit me. My sister Za'Maya sometimes came over too. She liked to play with cars. One time we were in the living room, and I was talking to Za'Maya. My mom thought she heard me say her name, but she shook her head. She didn't think it was possible for me to know my sister who had passed.

My mother was washing dishes while Za'Maya and I were having car races with the remote control. I drove my little purple car so hard it hit the wall. My mom turned around and saw me going to pick up the car and said, "Wait. Who are you talking to?"

I shrugged my shoulders like it was no big deal and said, "Za'Maya and I are playing cars."

My mom looked at me real serious like. "How do you know about Za'Maya, Tia?"

I set down the remote and looked at Mom like she was crazy. "She's my sister."

My mother was surprised I knew her name. She never told me about Za'Maya, who was one of the babies she had given birth to but had died before me.

But my mother wanted proof, so she said, "Za'Maya, if you are really here, show me."

And right then, a little purple car rushed into the kitchen and bumped into her foot.

My mother started crying because she knew my sister was actually right there in the room with us.

"It's OK, Mom. It's just Za'Maya."

My mother stood there frozen. I hadn't used the remote control. She looked at the car and at me and back at the car and called out my sister's name.

"Za'Maya?"

"Yes, Mom. I told you we was playing cars."

My mother started to tear up. I didn't know why Za'Maya would make her so sad. I always had fun whenever I played with her.

My mother came into the living room and sat down with me.

"Who else do you play with, Tia?"

I was so happy that my mom finally wanted to meet all my

Chapter 7

friends. I said all their names so she would know they were real and that I wasn't pretending.

"I play mainly with Grandma Dolpha, but sometimes Za'Maya, Jaden, and Amir come over too."

My mom kept listening.

"Who else, baby?"

"Um, I think that's it. No. Wait. Sometimes Grandpa visits too."

My mom sat there with tears rolling down her cheeks. I thought she would be happy for me that I had friends. But she looked sad, so I gave her a hug.

"It's OK, Mom. They're nice to me."

My mom cried hard as she held me. It was true. I was seeing my family who had passed, only they seemed real to me. I mean, they are real to me. I can see them and hear them and play with them. So I was confused about why my mom would be crying.

"Tia, you play with them every day?"

I looked down at the cars. They weren't moving anymore. I guess Za'Maya went home.

"Sometimes. Not every day, though. Grandma Dolpha comes the most. But I think they're gone now. Is that OK?"

My mom hugged me again.

"Yes, baby. That's OK. I am just surprised that you know all their names. Did you know I lost three babies before you were born? Your sister Za'Maya, who you play with, and your brothers Jaden and Amir."

I was confused. I thought they were real.

"Are they angels now, Mom?"

My mother nodded. "Yes, they are angels now, Tia. But I am glad they visit you. Thank you for telling me. I wasn't sure what was going on. Sometimes I would walk in, and you would be talking, and your Barbies would be in all these different positions."

I giggled. "Grandma Dolpha says they need to stretch to keep their bodies young. So they did yoga last week. Is that OK, Mom?"

My mother held me close and whispered softly in my ear. "Of course it's OK. I was just worried because I didn't know who you were playing with. Or why toys were moving on their own."

"It's OK, Mom. They're playing too. You don't need to be scared. They're nice to me. And they love you very much. Grandma Dolpha tells me that all the time. She says she's proud of you and that she's here with you every day."

Then my mom cried harder, and I sat there with her. Sometimes you just need to be with someone when they're sad. Words can get in the way. So I just put my head on her lap and fell asleep as she stroked my hair and cried.

Tea Parties

I had lots of tea parties with Grandma Dolpha, too. Now that my mom knew she was real, we invited her to have tea with us.

Chapter 7

Sometimes, my mom would come, but she said the chairs were uncomfortable, so she would sit on the floor.

"Can you see her, Mom? She's sitting right next to you."

My mother looked to her side. "Who?"

"Grandma Dolpha. She's right there."

I pointed, but my mother said she couldn't see her. Then she took her little teacup and pretended to take a sip, just like me and Grandma Dolpha do.

"Mom, would you like a cookie?"

There was a tiny plate filled with pretend cookies that we were eating, and Grandma Dolpha reminded me to ask my mom if she wanted some.

I watched as my mom looked at me and the empty chair across from me. As she took another pretend sip of tea, she said, "Yes, Tia. I would love one."

Rebuking the Devil

Everyone has a guardian angel. Grandma Dolpha is one of mine. She's always with me, and if I get scared, she tells me I'm going to be OK. Some nights I cough real hard, and blood comes up, and I start to wheeze.

One time it got so bad; I was coughing up a lot of blood. I asked her if I was going to die, and she said, "No, Tia. You're gonna be just fine."

As soon as she said that, my mom came in and wiped the

blood from my mouth softly while my dad put on my oxygen. And Grandma Dolpha was right. I fell asleep peacefully while my mom held me close and Grandma Dolpha sang.

. . .

I remember another time Grandma Dolpha woke me up in the middle of the night.

"Tia, Tia."

I was real sleepy, so she had to say it again.

"Tia, Tia. Wake up. Can you hear me?"

I yawned and stretched my arms and opened my eyes and saw Grandma Dolpha sitting on the end of my bed.

"Pray with me, Tia."

So I prayed with her. While we prayed, she told me, "This is how you rebuke the Devil."

My eyes got real wide. I wondered, was the Devil in my room?

"I have been praying for you since the day you were born. But I want you to help me. Can you do that now, Tia?"

I nodded. I always wanted to help Grandma Dolpha.

Then she said, "It's time you learned how. I will keep praying for you, Tia, but it's important that you start now, too. The more people that pray, the stronger the prayer becomes. Did you know that?"

I shook my head. I didn't know that's how prayer worked.

Chapter 7

Grandma Dolpha said, "Whenever something comes to hurt you, if you pray to God and tell the Devil to leave, then the Devil has to leave."

That night, the Devil was right there in my room and trying real hard to take me. Grandma Dolpha woke me up to show me how to rebuke the Devil while she was telling him to leave.

Together we both prayed hard. I couldn't see him, but I knew something was wrong. The room was darker than it was supposed to be, and my chest started to hurt. All the lights in the house, even the nightlights, were out. And it was supposed to be a full moon, but there was a shadow over the moon, so no light was coming through the windows. Grandma Dolpha says when there's a shadow over the moon, that means trouble.

So now, whenever I feel something is wrong, whether it's with me, a friend, or someone in my family, I pray hard and rebuke the Devil so he can't hurt me or the other person. Grandma Dolpha tells me to keep my faith and to always pray, so I do.

God's Reveal!

One time Miss B. and I both saw Grandma Dolpha at school! I don't know why she was there, but she came right up to us and, for some reason, asked me and Miss B. where the office was. I pointed toward the main building and told Miss B., "That's Grandma Dolpha!"

A Child of Faith

Miss B. took a picture, and then Grandma Dolpha disappeared! We looked under the trailer where my classroom was, and there was nothing under the trailer. We walked around the trailer, and there was nothing there, either. The sun was so bright that we had trouble seeing the main building where the office was. We kept looking, but we didn't see the woman in the long skirt and red sweater anywhere.

But what we did have was proof! We could show my mother this time! Miss B. and I both saw her, and Grandma Dolpha was in the same outfit. I don't know why, but she always wears the same clothes. She likes to wear a red sweater with a long black skirt, and her hair is always pulled back in a ponytail. And she wears this bright red lipstick. I think she's pretty, like my mom, so I don't mind if she doesn't change her outfit.

When we got home, Miss B. and I showed my mother the photo on her phone. There was all this bright golden light around her, but you could still tell it was Grandma Dolpha. My mom kept staring at the picture. She couldn't believe Grandma Dolpha was at school.

"What and how was my mama doing at your school? She's been deceased since 1997. You said she wanted to go to the front office?"

"Yes, ma'am."

My mother sat with that for a moment. Miss B. and I couldn't explain why Grandma Dolpha was at school. Maybe she was there to talk to the lady who kept quiet about the bad

Chapter 7

nurse? I hope she found her. Knowing Grandma Dolpha, she already knew where the office was; she was just playing a game with me and wanted to let Miss B. play, too.

Chapter 8

My Speech and My Message

I talk to angels. Sometimes they come to me in prayer. But they come when I'm not praying, too. I talk to Jesus and God more now that I'm older. If I ask a question, they show me a sign, like an angel visiting and praying for me, or they give me a vision in my dreams before something happens so I know what to do.

—Tia'Ahlee Maxie

Each time I flatline, I see Jesus, God, and my angels. I remember each time with Jesus like it just happened. There is always this bright gold light, and I feel so safe and comforted, even though everything going on around me is probably very different for others when I am with Jesus. The third time I flatlined, I was fourteen. I was coughing up a lot of blood, and my parents rushed me to the hospital. I spent a lot of time in the ICU.

When I was coughing up blood this time and I flatlined, I remember I was on the floor and feeling real tired. I kept hearing my mom cry. And I said, "What's happening? What's wrong?"

My parents kept looking at me like they were very scared. They wouldn't tell me. I wasn't sure why they were keeping a secret.

Then I said, "Mom, I'm sleepy."

And I heard my mom say, "No! Stay with us!"

And then my dad said, "No, Tia! Stay here!"

And I'm like, what do you mean stay with you? And then I saw angels that were really pretty, and one looked like a young Grandma Dolpha. Another was one of my great-great-grandmothers. And then I saw Jesus and this bright gold light. I asked them, "Am I dying?"

And they said, "No. You are going to be OK." And then I giggled, because Jesus makes me happy.

I don't know if my parents see me giggle or if it is just for Jesus. Once I see my angels and Jesus, I am comforted. The bright light is so warm and loving. It is very nice in Heaven. It is such a beautiful place, and I know that when it is my time, I will go there to be with Grandma Dolpha, all my other family members who have passed, God and Jesus, and all my angels. My grandma Dolpha looks like me and my mom. We both are

Chapter 8

part of her, and she is so proud of my mother for having me and taking such good care of me and my family. And when my mom gets sad, Grandma Dolpha reminds me to tell her that.

When I flatline and I am in Heaven, there is a part of me that wants to stay because it is so nice there, and I don't have any pain or discomfort. But I always do what Jesus says, and when it is time for me to come back, I do. When I come back, it's a little weird, because I am confused, and at first, I'm wondering what happened. And then either the doctor tells me, or my mother and my father tell me what happened. And then I remember where I am and am happy to be back.

People sometimes ask me if I am scared when I flatline. The best way I can explain it is after I have chest pain—like this time when I was coughing up a lot of blood and spent some time in the ICU—I pass out, so I don't really know what is happening around me. But right before I pass out, I am very scared, because I don't know if it is my time yet.

I'm not going to kid you. When I am struggling to breathe right before it happens, it is very scary. It's different from having a stuffy nose or a cough. Way different. Like, scary different. I don't know if you have ever experienced not being able to breathe before, but it is terrifying because you can't control it, no matter how much you want to. Your throat closes up and your chest gets real tight. Then your lungs don't work and you start to turn blue. Even your tongue changes color, but you don't notice that because you're gasping for air—but none comes. You can't talk or cry. Everything just shuts down. And that's when your heart stops, and you collapse, and you think you've died.

But when I pass out and flatline, I think it might be scarier for my parents and my sister, Le Le, because they have to stay and watch over me. I worry about my mother, especially because it is very hard on her when this happens. I know it's scary for my dad and sister, too. But my dad has to be brave for all of us.

I have had some close calls when my parents thought I was going to flatline, like when we were at a hotel in Houston right before I went to the doctor recently and started coughing up lots of blood. But Grandma Dolpha came and told me I was going to be OK, and I told my dad that. Then I yelled so my mother could hear me from the bathroom: "It's OK. Grandma Dolpha is here. She says I'm going to be OK!"

I can't see my mother when I tell her these things, but I hope it helps her feel better. I know she's crying when I am in there or when she steps away sometimes when I am in the hospital. She doesn't want me to see her sad or crying, but I know she is sad and worrying about me. But I don't want her to be sad, because I am grateful to be here every day. I love my family so much and feel that every day is a blessing. Each morning when I wake up, I may forget I am blessed in that moment, but something always reminds me to give thanks by the end of the day, because each day we have on this Earth is precious, whether we realize it or not.

Chapter 8

Praying for Others

They took an MRI of my heart at Texas Children's Hospital after my third flatline. Once I was stabilized, they said I would need another surgery. When I was waiting for surgery, I kept looking at this woman who looked very scared. Grandma Dolpha kept telling me to go talk to her, but I was like, "I don't know her." And Grandma Dolpha kept saying, "She needs you. Her daughter is in surgery. Go pray with her."

I told my mom what Grandma Dolpha said and asked her if it would be OK if I prayed with the Muslim lady who was scared,

This Muslim woman's daughter was having surgery. I asked if we could pray together.

and my mom said yes. Even though I was nervous, I walked up to the woman and told her, "Hi, my name is Tia. My guardian angel told me to come pray with you. She says your daughter is having surgery. Would it be OK if we prayed together?"

The woman looked up at me, and tears ran down her face. She nodded, and I took her hands in mine and began to pray with her. After we prayed together, she said she wanted to know my God, so I went back over to where my mother was, got my Bible, and gave it to her. She thanked me and said, "I was very scared, and you gave me peace about my daughter. I believe you when you say she is going to be OK. Thank you for your prayer."

After I prayed with the lady, I went back and sat down with my mother. I was the last one to go in for surgery that day. My mother says she saw Grandma Dolpha while she was waiting for me. My mother was crying and praying at the same time, so Grandma Dolpha came to comfort her, just as she had told me to comfort the lady who was worried about her own daughter. The surgery took several hours, but my mom kept praying, and so did Grandma Dolpha.

When I was in surgery, my doctor noticed one of my BT shunts was clotted up, so when they went in, both of my largest collateral veins had collapsed. I had created so many collateral veins that it became almost impossible to breathe, so they wrapped them in titanium alloy to prevent them from clotting up my shunts.

Chapter 8

When I came out of surgery, my heart doctor came out to let my mom know I was OK and that he would let her know when it was OK to come see me. After what seemed like forever, a nurse came and waved my mom inside the ICU so she could be with me. When my doctor made his rounds and found her in the room with me, he told her about the surgery and what he did with my bi-directional glenn. Then he told her that the MRI showed that I had so many collateral veins that he could not do any more operations or I would bleed out.

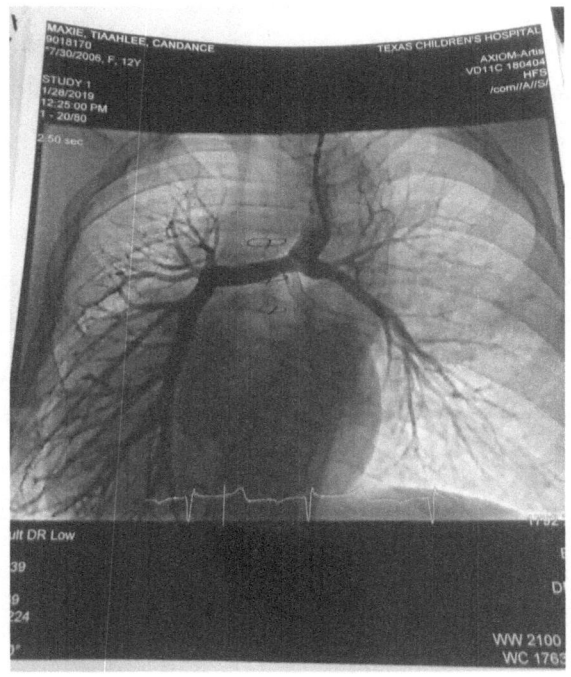

Notice how my lungs and heart are on the right side of my body instead of the left.

A Child of Faith

When he told us that, I could see my mother was scared. I was too. Then the doctor explained that my heart has to work harder than a normal person's because of all my medical conditions and that the collateral veins kept growing so I could get more oxygen. But so many grew that it was like they were choking me. He told Mom about how he wrapped them in titanium to keep them closer together. And then he said now we would have to manage my heart condition with medication because we couldn't do any more surgeries.

At first, I was scared when he said that. But then my mom looked at the MRI images and said the veins looked like two hands reaching skyward to God and that God would help me breathe. That made me feel a lot better, because Jesus and God were always helping me.

When my mom told our doctor about my two hands reaching to God for air, he understood this because he is the kind of doctor who prays. My mom says she only wants doctors who pray and believe in God. This is important to me and my family. We are a family of faith and want to be surrounded by God's love always, not just at home or when we sleep but also whenever we go to the doctor or hospital or do something basic like ride in the car or buy groceries.

Chapter 8

Special Visitors

My mom and I have seen angels in our house before. When we see them, they visit at night. The first time it happened, my sister and my dad were asleep. I woke up because I was coughing. This happens a lot, so I am used to it. My mother gave me some medicine to help with my cough so I could go back to sleep. Then she went back to bed. But when I came out of the bathroom, I heard sandals walking down the hallway.

I ran into my parents' bedroom and told them about the sandals. My mother said she wasn't sure whether to get the bat or the gun, so she grabbed a baseball bat and waited. I wasn't scared, though. I knew it was probably something good. I told my mom she didn't need the bat, but she held on to it just in case. As we were walking down the hall, we saw something glowing brightly. Slowly, we turned the corner, and there was this giant angel. My mother and I couldn't believe it. We just looked at each other and then at the angel. Its wings were so high, hanging way over the chair. The angel was sitting down and praying. So I started praying too. And I stared at her for a long time, but I didn't say anything. I didn't want to interrupt the angel's praying.

When I looked at my mom, she nudged me like we should go back to bed and let the angel pray. When we turned to go back down the hall, the angel turned around and looked right at Mom. I didn't see a face. My mother was scared. She said the angel's face was blurry, just made of bright white light. I thought the angel was pretty. I have never seen such a bright, clear light before, except when I was in Heaven. It was so beautiful and peaceful.

When we were leaving to go back down the hall, I couldn't tell if it was a woman or a man angel. My mom said when it looked at her and raised up, she could tell it was a woman. I wanted to talk to the angel to see if she would talk to me. And I wanted to touch her, too. But I was afraid if I touched her, I would die, since sometimes angels come to take you, so I didn't reach out to her.

Unlike my mother, I am used to seeing angels. If you have seen angels, you are probably used to them too. If I see something I don't want to, I go around it. Or if I feel a bad spirit or am scared, I rebuke it as my grandma Dolpha taught me.

Different angels that we don't know come to our house whenever they need to pray for me or my family. One time it was a man angel. I saw him on the couch before I went to bed. He was praying real hard. His wings were so big they spread out over the whole back of the couch. I showed my mother, and she saw him too. This time she wasn't scared, because the last time nothing bad happened. She knows that angels are real and understands they are here to pray for us. So she likes it when they visit now. It is a comfort to know they are with us and helping us with their prayers.

Chapter 9

The Testimony of God

Our Father who art in heaven,
hallowed be thy name.
Thy kingdom come.
Thy will be done
on earth as it is in heaven.
Give us this day our daily bread,
and forgive us our trespasses,
as we forgive those who trespass against us,
and lead us not into temptation,
but deliver us from evil.
For thine is the kingdom, and the power, and the glory,
forever and ever.
Amen.

—The Lord's Prayer

A Child of Faith

The fourth time I flatlined, I was fifteen. I remember I was coughing and fighting for air and called out to my parents before I collapsed in my bathroom. My mom called 911. While she and my dad were waiting, they were praying over me and crying and taking turns doing CPR. My mom says when the paramedics came, they did CPR on me for less than ten minutes. Then they stopped and walked out of the bathroom to where my parents were waiting. One of the paramedics took his index finger and dragged it across his throat to show them I had died.

My parents started crying. *How could they lose me?*

I'm so glad they refused to give up. Both of them went into the bathroom, and my mom started doing CPR over me while my daddy started praying. Then when my mom got tired, my daddy did CPR, and my mom was praying to Jesus for me to come back. When my daddy got tired, my mom took over doing CPR again while my daddy prayed. And they kept taking turns doing CPR and praying. And after ten minutes of prayer and CPR from my parents, I came back.

I remember waking up confused and coughing. I didn't know what was going on when they were doing CPR on me, because I was with Jesus and my angels while all that was happening. I was in the golden light, being comforted while my parents were fighting to keep me alive.

When I woke up, my parents were so relieved and stopped doing CPR. The paramedics were still there waiting outside as

Chapter 9

if it was over. When my parents came out of the bathroom and told them I was still alive, the paramedics both looked at each other in disbelief and walked into the bathroom. They said, "How? How is she alive?"

And my mother and father said, "Because we did CPR. Because we prayed. And because we never gave up or lost faith."

The paramedics were about to put oxygen on me and take me to the hospital.

But my mother said, "No."

The paramedics looked confused.

So my mother said, "You're not taking my baby. You gave up on her. What if she dies in the ambulance? Will you give up on her then, too? No, sir. We're taking our baby. You can follow us, though."

My parents put me in the car and drove to the hospital without waiting for the ambulance. The ambulance followed my parents, but my mom still beat them, like she did when I was a baby when she drove to Texas Children's Hospital. They probably thought it was strange that my parents wouldn't want me to go in the ambulance with the oxygen, but my mom knows best, so she and my daddy drove me straight to the ER.

When we got to the hospital, the ER doctors checked my vitals and said I was stable. We were all relieved. They said I would be OK, and they sent me home and told me to sleep with my oxygen on all night. That night, my mom slept with me. She said she couldn't really sleep. Instead, she watched over me and prayed the rest of the night until my angels told her it was OK to rest, and then she finally did.

The Power of Prayer

When I flatlined that last time, I asked God if I was going to die, and He said, "No, Tia. It is not your time." I was happy because I wanted to spend more time with my family. When they said it wasn't my time, I wanted to leave right away and go home. But my angels comforted me with their soft wings and told me to wait. I guess that might have been when my parents were praying and doing CPR on me.

My apostle says prayer is the best medicine, and I believe him. He and his wife pray for me and help me heal all the time. So do God, Jesus, my parents, my sister, and all my angels. They all pray for me so much, just like I pray for them. Prayer is special, because it saved me when I flatlined that night, and it has saved me many other times, too.

You may be thinking that's because I have angels. But it's not just me who has angels. You have them too. God and Jesus are there for you too. So are your family and your loved ones who passed on, just like my grandma Dolpha. All you need to do is ask your family, loved ones, God, and your angels, and they will comfort and pray for you, too.

I always pray for my family and others. Sometimes, when someone hurts my feelings, I pray for them, too. Everyone needs prayer. One of my prayers has been to write this book. I never thought it would happen, because I was having so many health problems, and I didn't know any publishers. But one time, when I was at the doctor's, I told them I wanted to write a book about my story to help other kids who may have heart problems or cancer or some other condition and who are being bullied about being different. I don't think anyone should suffer for being different. When you are made different, it is for a reason. It makes you special. And I truly believe I am here to help other people like me learn that it is OK to be different and to help them not feel so alone.

Make-A-Wish

When my doctors heard this, they wrote to the Make-A-Wish Foundation in Sugar Land, Texas. My mother told me to not get too excited, because not everyone gets their wish, but I prayed real hard, and God told me not to worry. That it would happen. So, every day, I told my family that I was going to write a book. I even told Apostle Mitchell and his wife. I couldn't wait to get started on my book. It's hard not to be excited when you know your wish is about to come true!

Then one day, we got a letter in the mail from Miss Shelly at Make-A-Wish. Mom opened it up and started reading it to me. We both started crying. It was real! My wish had been granted! I was going to write a book!

A Child of Faith

When I learned my wish had come true, I told our apostle I was so excited that I started running as fast as I could. And I normally can't run, but that day Jesus gave me extra oxygen. My apostle yelled out to the entire church: "Y'all should be running around the church like Tia! Look at her go!"

My parents were laughing, and so were the other kids and my sister. It was a very special moment for me and my family, and I am so glad I got to share it with my church and pastor and apostle, too.

Over the past few years, I and my family have gotten to know Miss Shelly. I love her so much, because she is a very good person and really cares about me. Sometimes she visits to see how I am doing. Sometimes she calls. And sometimes she FaceTimes. I always like to spend time with her because she is helping me. She is my wish fairy.

Miss Shelly has a daughter named Piper, who is really good friends with my younger sister, Le Le. Whenever Miss Shelly calls, Piper and Le Le like to say hi to each other too.

One time, we got to go to Make-A-Wish to visit Miss Shelly and Miss Diana. It was very special, because Miss Shelly took us around and showed us other wishes that had been granted. There were lots of wishes with their unique stories on the walls. Some kids wanted to be a fireman. Others wanted to meet stars like Beyoncé or visit Disney World. All of these are very good wishes. And now, mine was coming true, and it was very exciting to visit the place that was making it all happen.

Chapter 9

My sister and I visited Make-A-Wish.

A Child of Faith

Le Le and I met Miss Diana (left), the writer who worked on this book with me, and Miss Shelly (right), who works for Make-A-Wish and helps make so many dreams come true.

When we were there, Miss Shelly asked me which wall I wanted my wish to go on, and I wasn't sure. I'm still thinking about it, because they have so many good places to show your wishes. And I want to make sure I pick a wall where the most people will see it so they will be inspired just like me.

One part of my wish is to go on a talk show on TV to talk about my book. Miss Shelly is working on that wish for me, too. I hope it happens, because then I will reach even more

Chapter 9

people who can hear my story and feel less alone. And if they have lost their faith, maybe my story will help them get it back.

I know that God made this wish possible because He wants me to tell my story. I prayed real hard for it to come true, and I give thanks every day because here I am, talking to you and sharing what happened and how I am using my gift to help others.

I have another wish, and I'm not sure when it will happen, but I also want to make a doll for kids like me who have had open-heart surgeries. I took one of my dolls that has my hair and my color, and I put stitches on its chest so it would look just like me.

The doll I want to make for other people will look like me and have stitches on its chest, a glowing heart, and a superhero cape with the letter T on the back for Tia. And it will have all kinds of things to go with it, like a small oxygen tank, a wheelchair, a medication bag, and an inhaler. Oh, and a kitty, like Shadow and Rody, because kitties are special too.

I also want to have a clothing line—"A Child of Faith"—with T-shirts, superhero capes, and other things that kids like me can wear to remind them to keep their faith, no matter how hard life is sometimes. It's important to always have faith, and it begins with you. So trust in God and pray. Keep your faith, because it is a very special gift from God that is always yours to keep.

Part 3

And Grace My Fears Relieved

I sought the Lord, and he answered me;

he delivered me from all my fears.

—**Psalm 34:4, NIV**

Chapter 10

Do Not Let Your Hearts Be Troubled

When people ask me if I'm scared since I have so many medical conditions, I tell them, "Sometimes. But it doesn't matter if I'm scared. I'm not going to quit. Or the Devil will win."

—Tia'Ahlee Maxie

My mom says I am a walking miracle.

I am her first baby who lived. I have had four open-heart surgeries, thirteen heart caths, more BT shunts than I can count, and several emergency procedures. I have flatlined four times. The first time I was just six months old. My baseline oxygen is 60 percent, which makes it *very* hard to breathe. I cough up blood often and have fluid buildup in my lungs. Now, we go to Houston a few times a week for specialty care, where I

A Child of Faith

have the fluid drained. Sometimes I also go to the doctor in my hometown for non-emergencies, like if I need cough medicine or a new inhaler. I have very good doctors who take care of me, so I know I will be OK.

I know I should wear my oxygen and glasses more often at school, but I get teased, and it hurts my feelings. Now, I am shy about wearing my glasses in school, even though I sit way in the back and have trouble seeing unless the teacher writes at the top of the chalkboard. I can hear her OK, but I don't see very well. When I first got my glasses, the kids at school teased me and said I looked like a bug or an alien. It really hurt my feelings, so now I don't wear them at all. Maybe once in a while, if my eyes hurt. But as soon as I can, I take them off. I am the same way with my oxygen. Some kids at school can be mean, and they would tease me about being in a wheelchair and using oxygen. It would hurt my feelings because I can't help that I need oxygen and can't walk very far.

When you don't have a heart condition or other illness, it is hard to understand what others are going through. And some kids are so uncomfortable with who they are that they make fun of people like me just to make themselves feel better. I shouldn't let them do this, but I don't want to get in trouble at school. So now, I sneak my glasses on in the back of the classroom when I need to see and ask my nurse to take me outside when I need to use my oxygen.

I have had issues with digestion since I was a baby. I was

Chapter 10

on PediaSure until last year. When I was six months old, my mother's grandma snuck me some food. My mom says when she came in, my great-grandma was tapping my leg and singing church hymns. At the time, my mother was working hard to keep up with the bills. She says when she walked in, her grandma was humming the Lord's Prayer, and I was eating the bowl of mashed potatoes and giggling.

My mom said she couldn't believe it. She asked her grandma what she made, and her grandma said, "Just mashed potatoes. No salt, no gravy. She loves it. Look."

I had potatoes all over my face and all in my hair, but I was eating! My mom was so happy. She started giving me some regular food with the PediaSure, but I still needed the PediaSure to supplement what I was eating until I turned fifteen.

My favorite food now is soul food. I really like ribs, greens, and potatoes. All the stuff that my mom makes, because she makes it with love, and it tastes real good. I like it when we all eat as a family. They are happy times, and we talk about our day.

Sometimes I tell my family about my dreams for the future. I want to have kids one day. I also want to go to college and learn how to write graphic novels. Even though my mom tells me I'm on borrowed time, I still think I can do these things. I also want to write more books. I really like graphic novels. I also like to draw. I think that's why I like graphic novels so much, because they are like books with cartoons that make the characters come alive as soon as you draw them.

A Child of Faith

Once, I wrote a short book called *Super Heart* for my friend Keyarra. She is my best friend, and she has heart problems too. And so does a lady I met at Chick-fil-A. At first, I thought I was the only person who had heart problems, and I was sad. But now I have met other people who have heart problems like me, so I don't feel so alone anymore. The book I wrote called *Super Heart* is about heart surgery. I talk about how our hearts are special, and other people like me end up meeting each other and working with each other to fight crime. We are superheroes with good hearts, and because we have good hearts, we can battle the bad people and save the good people so they don't have to be sad or alone anymore.

Dr. Jesus

I know I've told you a lot about different times I've been in the hospital, but I have one more I want to share with you before we finish our conversation. One time, when I was six years old, an angel came and visited me in the hospital. It was a man angel, and he was with Jesus.

They came when I was in surgery, and I was asleep during the operation. I was scared and had a bad feeling like I was going to die, and I remember I kept saying, "I don't want to die. I don't want to die." It's like I could see the surgery as it was happening. And then I looked closer at who was doing the surgery, and it was Jesus! He looked the same as when I went to

Chapter 10

Heaven and He showed me around. He was doing the surgery and said, "Don't worry, Tia. I am the surgeon. I'm doing all your surgeries. The doctors are not. The doctors are here, but I am your surgeon."

I kept watching from high up above as the doctors assisted Jesus. I noticed Jesus was doing something with my heart, like giving it a massage. Jesus told me to go back to sleep and that when I woke up, all would be well. I felt at peace after He said that, so I went back to sleep.

And when I woke up, I was OK. I told my family that Jesus was the doctor! And they were very happy. This is why my mom always wants a doctor who prays. That way, Jesus can guide the doctor and take over if He needs to. I had to rest for a few days in the hospital after that, and when we got home, I noticed there were all these white spirits flying around the house. I asked them what they wanted, and they said they were healing angels to make sure I would recover quickly.

Maybe you will want to get a doctor who prays. That way, Dr. Jesus can do your surgeries, too. He does a really good job and will protect you if you ask Him to—just like He did that time I was really scared because I was having another surgery. I know it's still not fun to be in the hospital, but it feels a lot better when you know Jesus is helping.

A Child of Faith

Dreaming with Grandma Dolpha

I don't know if you dream about angels. If not, maybe you will start dreaming about them after you finish this book. I have many angels who visit me in my dreams. Sometimes they look like real people, like Grandma Dolpha. Sometimes I just see this bright golden light. Regardless of what they look like, they are always there to comfort me. And your angels will do the same for you.

My grandma Dolpha visits me a lot in my dreams. And the dreams always feel so real. I remember one time, I was dreaming we were at Aunt Betty's, and Grandma Dolpha woke me up and told me to come find her. She was out in the woods and told me she was really alive. I told her to come with me so I could show her to everyone. But she said she couldn't, that she had to stay there. So I ran to the house and told Aunt Betty and my mom and everyone to come with me. And we all ran out to the woods, but we couldn't find Grandma Dolpha. I told them she was just there, and I even pointed to the spot where she was. But they weren't mad or anything. They just said, "It's OK, Tia. Maybe she had to go."

Then my dream changed, and I was back at my house. My mom was cooking soul food, and Grandma Dolpha woke me up and said, "Tia, Tia! Do you smell all that good food?"

And I was like, "Yes, Grandma Dolpha, I do! Let's go get some!"

And Grandma Dolpha said, "Now you know I'm alive. Right, Tia?"

Chapter 10

I smiled and nodded, and Grandma Dolpha chuckled.

Then she said, "I can't go with you in the kitchen right now, Tia. You go on now and eat, and I'll be right here when you get back."

At first, I didn't want to go without Grandma Dolpha, but she smiled real big, so I got up and went into the kitchen and ate a big plate of soul food with my family.

After we ate, I asked to be excused and rushed back to my room. This time Grandma Dolpha was there sitting on my bed, and she was smiling. She gave me such a big hug, I felt so happy, and then I fell back asleep.

Then I started crying in my dream because I wanted to see Grandma Dolpha. I never got to meet her in person because she died of cancer before I was born, but I knew she would come if I had a lucid dream. I was twelve years old, and I remember I was crying in my dream for Grandma Dolpha to come.

Then I heard, "Tia, Tia."

At first, I thought it was my mom.

But then I heard the voice again. It was louder this time: "Tia, Tia, get up. Get up, baby. Get up. Your Grandma Dolpha is right here."

In my dream, I woke up and sat up in bed, and it really was Grandma Dolpha! I gave her such a big hug; it made her so happy.

"I don't have much time, Tia. It's almost morning."

I was about to cry because I didn't want her to leave, but

then she said, "I love you so much, and I just want to tell you that I will always be with you. Just be a good girl. Listen to your mommy. She loves you so much."

I was trying not to cry, but I was kinda upset because I could tell she was in a hurry to go.

Then she said, "Don't be upset. Be happy that I tell you this. Everything's going to be OK. I gotta go back. I love you. Now when you wake up, I want you to remember that I love you and your mom. Be sure to tell her how proud I am of her. Will you do that for me, Tia?"

I nodded as Grandma Dolpha wiped the tears from my cheek. Then she gave me a kiss and a hug and said, "Now get your rest and go back to sleep."

She helped me get back into bed and pulled the covers over me so I wouldn't get cold. It all felt so real. I even saw her walk out of my room. I closed my eyes and fell back asleep.

That morning, I woke up in my room, and I was confused. I thought I saw my grandma, but she wasn't there. I sat up in bed and called out for her. "Grandma Dolpha! Grandma Dolpha! Where are you?"

My mother ran in and asked, "What's wrong, baby? Were you calling for your grandma?"

I started crying. "Yes, Mom. She was just here. Is she in the front room?"

My mother shook her head. "No, Tia. She's deceased."

And then I told her what Grandma Dolpha told me to say, and then it was two of us who were crying.

Chapter 11

My Peace I Give to You

Peace I leave with you; my peace I give to you. I do not give to you as the world gives. Do not let your hearts be troubled, and do not be afraid.

—John 14:27, NIV

I have been bullied and threatened most of my life by people who think they can get away with bad things because I am different from them. I am here to tell you that different is OK. Everyone is different. Some of us just show it more on the outside than others. I have a wheelchair, oxygen, and a nurse. Other people may have cancer and lose their hair. Maybe someone else is sad and needs medication. Whatever kind of different you are, it's OK. Please know that you are loved by God and that He made you special because you can handle it.

God made me special by giving me a pure heart. I'm not saying it's easy being different, because sometimes it's not. For example, I don't understand why some people don't want to be my friend. It makes me sad. I am nice to people, but they aren't always nice to me. Sometimes they take advantage of me, and I let them because I don't wanna start trouble. So I just let them do what they want. I wanna be nice. I don't wanna be mean, because God is always nice.

But my parents are teaching me to stand up for myself because God doesn't want me to be sad or abused. So I am working on doing that more. It is hard for me to do that, because it is not my way. But now, when my mother asks me if something is going on, I have to tell her because she won't stop asking until I finally tell her. She knows how I am. I keep a lot inside. Maybe you do too.

When some kids tease me and make me feel bad or ashamed, sometimes I want to tell them off, but I know that I can't do that. That would make me mean like them, so I just pray about it. Or sometimes I just tell them, "God doesn't pick on people. You don't know your future. You could end up like this too." And then they get real quiet.

Sometimes I wonder if the mean people are upset that I get special attention at school. I really don't know why they would be. They are not the ones who are in wheelchairs or struggling to breathe. But God tells me not to worry. He says I should focus on the good things in the world. So I am noticing the nice people more, too.

Educating Others

Sometimes kids and teachers ask why I am in a wheelchair, because they are curious. I tell them I have low oxygen and that I was born with a heart condition. If I say I was born with heart disease, they will ask if I got it, like it was something you could catch. And I say no. I was born this way. Then I explain that my heart is on my right side instead of my left side and that I used to get in trouble during the Pledge of Allegiance because my teacher thought I was making fun of the flag when I was really just participating with everyone else.

Some people will ask me what low oxygen means. I tell them my oxygen is low. It's at 60 percent, so I can't walk or run around the whole school, or I get tired or pass out. Most people have oxygen that is close to 100 percent, and those people can walk and run and not pass out if they exercise. I explain this, and then they start to understand more.

There are some who ask more questions, and I tell them I am writing a book about my life, and they think it's cool. One of my teachers asked if she could buy a copy of my book when it gets published and if I could sign it. That made me happy. I told her, "Yes, ma'am," and I think that made her happy, too.

Making Friends

I used to think it was just me who was like this, because I didn't know anyone else who had heart problems. I used to feel ashamed because I was different. But when I asked God to show me other kids like me, He did. My best friend, Keyarra, told me that a lot of her friends used to leave her out, too. They wouldn't ask her over or to their birthday parties because she has a heart condition, and they didn't think she could do things. And I understood because that's just like how other people treat me. And I told her about the lady I met at Chick-fil-A who was born with heart problems like us and that she flatlined before when she was little too.

Talking to Keyarra about these things made me feel better, and it made her feel better, too. We understand each other, and this helps us be more comfortable with who we are. We are special and different from everyone else, but that's how God made us. When we play, we understand when one of us needs to take a break. Not all kids get that. But Keyarra does. I think it's important to have friends who understand you.

Sometimes I still feel ashamed because some of my friends don't really invite me to things. Maybe they think because of my heart condition I can't do anything, like parties and stuff. But I do like these things and wish they would ask me to hang out with them. I recently turned sixteen and invited my friends to my birthday party.

Some said they were coming, but they didn't come. So that

Chapter 11

showed me who my true friends were. I was looking forward to having lots of people there, and at first, I was upset. But the ones who didn't come showed their true colors, and it's important to know who your real friends are and who are not. One of my dad's friends is a singer, and he sang one of his songs that he wrote that I like, so that was nice. He performed it for me, and that was my favorite part of the party.

I also played on the swings at my party, and there was a little girl that looked just like my sister on the swing next to me. I really thought it was Le Le because she looked and acted just like her. But when I went inside, I found my sister. So I think

Me at my sixteenth birthday party

it was an angel who came to my party to make me feel better when some of the people I invited didn't come.

Keyarra is always nice to me, and she did come to my party. I like that we talk and understand each other. Keyarra and I sometimes have to rest. She gets it, so we spend time together at school and go to each other's birthday parties and things. And I am grateful to have her as my friend.

What Bullying Has Taught Me

People show who they are early on. For example, one time, I had a sleepover, and my favorite cousins came and brought their cousins with them. These other cousins had to leave the sleepover early because they were being mean and bossy. They were nice when they first came over, but pretty soon, I saw who they really were. It hurt my feelings because I was being nice to them, but they started being mean when my parents left the room.

My parents tell me to stop giving so much of myself to others and to start being good to myself. But I like to do things for people. Bullying has taught me to be nice to others, even if they aren't nice to me, because I never want someone to feel bad or left out. One time I felt bad for these kids in my neighborhood because they didn't have any toys. So I went to Walmart and got toys for them. After I gave them the toys, they went and told their parents I was being bossy and wouldn't let them play

Chapter 11

with my hoverboard. Then they started speaking to my sister and ignoring me, and I wondered why they were acting like that since it hurt my feelings.

But I don't let something like that stop me from being good or wanting to be nice to others. I know what it feels like to be sad or hurt. I have been bullied my whole life. It is painful, and I understand how hard it is. I want you to know that you don't have to take it.

How to Handle Bullies

If you are being bullied, please let someone you trust know what is happening. It could be your nurse, your doctor, the police, your parents, or a good friend. Please promise me you will tell someone. Don't keep quiet like I did all these years. It doesn't serve you, and it doesn't serve them.

When bullies say mean things, ignore them. They are not worth it. If they tease you, pray for them and walk away. Make sure you have a good support network and that you use it. If they hit you, tell someone who can help you. Prayer has helped me a lot. Pray to Jesus, and He will help you. Ask your angels for help, and they will come. God is always there for you. All you need to do is ask. Take comfort in your church and those who love and care about you.

Family Ties

It really makes me very upset when my family members say they love me and my sister but never talk to us or come see us, and then talk about the people we really, really love. It makes me mad when people think I'm stupid because I have a heart problem. There isn't anything wrong with me but my heart. Plus, I really want us to all get closer because life is too short, and my parents always say that. I really want our family members to just get along and stop fighting. So, come around the people you love because what you are fighting about is not worth it. And if they don't do it, then pray about it and let the good Lord take the wheel and be strong. Love yourself and trust Jesus always.

Be Your Own Superhero

I've always loved superheroes. I can't say I have a favorite because I like all of them—Superman, Wonder Woman, Batman, Spider-Man, and Black Panther—to me, they are all like angels in a way. They come swooping down and protect those who are in danger or need to be comforted. When they see ugly behavior, they stop it. They protect the good people and treat them with love and respect, and then the bullies are schooled on how they should behave.

You can be your own superhero by helping good people, being strong, and loving who you are. Don't let the bullies get

Chapter 11

to you. Keep treating people the way you want to be treated and live your best life. I know you can do it. God is on your side, and I am too!

Epilogue

Bright Shining as the Sun

So do not fear, for I am with you; do not be dismayed, for I am your God. I will strengthen you and help you; I will uphold you with my righteous right hand.

— Isaiah 41:10, NIV

Dear beautiful child of God,

I am happy you have read my book.

I hope my words comforted you and that you always feel the presence of the Lord in your life.

Any time you feel scared or worried, pray to God, and He will answer.

Any time you need comfort, ask your angels, and they will come.

A Child of Faith

Any time you feel ashamed, love yourself as you love your God.

And any time you feel bad, always remember that you are loved,

Always, forever, and beyond all measure.

—**Tia'Ahlee Maxie,
September 2022**

Appendix

Artwork, Poetry, and Photos

A Child of Faith

"A Mother's Love" by Sherricka Calvin

A mother's love is a gift from God.
Not a notion that can be easily taught.
It's like a cool breeze on a hot summer day
that whisks by to clean the stress from your thoughts.
A mother's love is so strong for her child
that not even a boulder could break it.
It's as if the heavens and the earth had created the bonding glue,
so that only the Lord above could shake it.
A mother's love is pure and natural
and comes strictly from the heart.
And with the love that Tia'Ahlee and I share,
this mother's love will NEVER BE BROKEN APART!
I love you, Tia'Ahlee Maxie.

Appendix

My family, 2023.
My mom and dad (back row), Sherricka and Pat, and (front row, left to right) my cousin Khloe, who recently came to live with us, me, and Le Le

This is a painting that I made in art class of "Christmas Road." I hung it on my bedroom wall.

A Child of Faith

I was a Jr. Pre-Teen finalist in the
2015 National American Miss Texas (NAM) Pageant.

The trophy I got for being first runner-up!

Appendix

Here's the official NAM certificate that I keep on my wall.

This is the tree where I collapsed and flatlined.

A Child of Faith

My sister, Le Le, all dressed up in her red tutu

Acknowledgments

First, I want to thank the good Lord for making me in His image. My faith in Him gives me strength and happiness every day. I also want to thank my mom and dad; my sister, Le Le; and my cousin Khloe. And my cats, Shadow and Rody. I love you all so much.

All my angels: Grandma Dolpha, Uncle Dietrich, Sister Za'Maya, Little Chris, Brother Jayden, and Brother Amir. My pastor and my apostle, I love you both so much. Aunt Benetha, Aunt Teegee, Aunt Betty, Aunt Lola, Aunty Elaine, Uncle Solomon, Uncle Jeremiah, a.k.a. Burger, Aunt Cheryl, Grandma Sadie, Grandma Isabel, Grandma Kathleen, Pawpaw Billydale, Miss Paulette, Aunt Monique, and Cousins Tiny, Roxy, Tameka Alexander, Serenity, Neesha, Colby, Dee, Shamiria, Neveah, John, Deydria, and Nini—thank you.

And many thanks to all the doctors and nurses who have taken care of me: Dr. Jeffrey Kim, Melissa Lewellyn, Nurse

A Child of Faith

Ashley, Dr. Jefferson, Nurse Cindy, Nurse Heather, Dr. Marlo Brawner, Dr. Chang, Dr. Chris, Dr. Mareke, Dr. Oleka, and Dr. Van Buren. And my good teachers: Mr. Moore, Miss Lewis, Miss Dana, Miss Tierney, Miss Kendell, Miss Jessica, and my ninth- and tenth-grade art teacher at LHS, Lufkin High School. My friends: Cadence, Keyarra, Aubrey, Shaley, Ray, Brianna, Sa'Nia, Brooklyn, and Mr. Jesse and his girlfriend, Cierra.

And Drs. Kim and Brawner and Nurse Cindy, who wrote to Make-A-Wish to help my dream of becoming a published author come true. That means the world to me, and this dream could not have come true without your help. I also want to thank Miss Shelly at Make-A-Wish and Miss Diana for allowing me the opportunity to write my first book and for visiting with me and giving me hope and strength, and for becoming my friend. And thank you to the awesome team at Greenleaf Book Group for publishing my book.

There are so many people who mean so much to me. If I forgot to include you, please know that I want to thank you, too. And lastly, I want to thank you for reading my book and for being here for me right when my wish came true.

Now it's your turn to make your wish!

About the Author

Tia'Ahlee Maxie is sixteen years old. She has a congenital heart condition that has challenged her throughout her life. Since birth, Tia has undergone extensive life-saving medical treatment, including four major open-heart surgeries, twelve heart caths, and thirteen emergency procedures to add BT shunts and stents. In 2021, she had a double titanium stent replacement to create more space in her chest so her heart could pump her blood more efficiently. The doctors have told her she cannot have any more surgeries, or she will bleed out

A Child of Faith

due to the extent of collateral veins her body has created to allow more oxygen to reach her brain.

In addition to fighting for her life each day, Tia is a survivor of physical, sexual, and emotional abuse. But she doesn't let any of this hold her back. Tia is a true child of faith who has always wanted to write a book to share her messages with others who may be struggling with their health or perhaps are in a similar situation with abuse or bullying. Tia enjoys spending time with her family and friends. Her faith and that of her family and the expert medical care she has received have enabled her to share her special message with you today. Tia's wish was made possible by Drs. Kim and Brawner and Nurse Cindy and the kind people at Make-A-Wish in Texas Gulf Coast and Louisiana, and Greenleaf Book Group in Austin, Texas. This is her first book. Tia lives in Lufkin, Texas, with her parents, Pat and Sherricka; her sister, Talia; her cousin Khloe; and their two cats, Shadow and Rody.

www.ingramcontent.com/pod-product-compliance
Lightning Source LLC
Chambersburg PA
CBHW030523080526
44586CB00011B/299